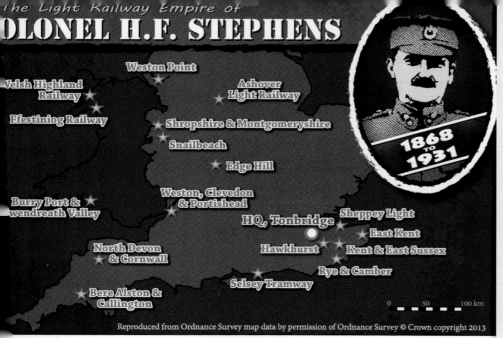

The Light Railway Empire of

OLONEL H.F. STEPHENS

1868 TO 1931

Weston Point
Welsh Highland Railway
Ashover Light Railway
Ffestiniog Railway
Shropshire & Montgomeryshire
Snailbeach
Edge Hill
Weston, Clevedon & Portishead
Burry Port & Gwendreath Valley
HQ, Tonbridge
Sheppey Light
East Kent
Hawkhurst
Kent & East Sussex
North Devon & Cornwall
Rye & Camber
Selsey Tramway
Bere Alston & Callington

0   50   100 km

Reproduced from Ordnance Survey map data by permission of Ordnance Survey © Crown copyright 2013

COLONEL STEPHENS SOCIETY

AUT...
Robi...
rjone...

PAG...
Book...

ADVERTISING:
Craig Amess
camess@mortons.co.uk

PUBLISHER:
Steve O'Hara

PUBLISHING DIRECTOR:
Dan Savage

COMMERCIAL DIRECTOR:
Nigel Hole

MARKETING MANAGER:
Charlotte Park
cpark@mortons.co.uk

PRINTED BY:
William Gibbons and Sons,
Wolverhampton

ISBN:
978-1-911639-05-3

PUBLISHED BY:
Mortons Media Group Ltd
Media Centre
Morton Way
Horncastle
Lincolnshire
LN9 6JR
Tel: 01507 529529

CONTENTS

R PICTURE: The Kent & East Sussex Railway's LBSCR 'Terrier' 0-6-0T No. 3 *Bodiam* climbs Tenterden Bank
y 9, 2006. ALAN CROTTY

Today's Kent & East Sussex Railway is the finest surviving example of the standard gauge light railways pioneered by Colonel Holman F Stephens, and an award-winning museum dedicated to him is located at Tenterden Town station. The Terrier Trust's LBSCR 0-6-0T No. 78 *Knowle*, running in British Railways livery as No. 32678, is seen crossing Hexden Channel bridge. In Stephens' day, second-hand 'Terriers' were to be found not only on this line but on other railways he managed. MARTIN CREESE/KESR

Colonel Holman Fred Stephens came at the opposite end of Britain's great railway building era to the likes of Richard Trevithick, George and Robert Stephenson and Isambard Kingdom Brunel, yet was just as much a larger-than-life engineering expert in the field.

The colonel was renowned for establishing a burgeoning portfolio of cheaply-built light railways serving a variety of purposes at remote and obscure locations such as Selsey, Leysdown-on-Sea, Camber Sands, Snailbeach and Ashover Butts. The established railways of the day knew they could never profit from these routes.

Built under the auspices of the 1896 Light Railways Act, many of his lines sought to connect rural communities that would otherwise have remained disenfranchised in perpetuity from the national network – which already served the country's cities, towns, industrial areas and ports, with no desire to explore the potential custom that remained in the shires.

Stephens used his engineering expertise and knack for finding cost-effective solutions to build local lines that could

Colonel Holman F Stephens. CSRM

yet be made to pay – second-hand locomotives, carriages and wagons running at no more than 25mph from and to minimalist stations. While Stephens set out to serve very much the lower end

of the market, his abilities were widely respected by senior figures in the rail industry of his day.

Benevolence to the inhabitants of remote and sparsely-populated areas was the outcome but by no means the intention; the colonel designed and built lines that were designed to turn in a profit.

They might have done just that had it not been for the dawn of the age of road motor transport, which broke around 75 years after the Stockton & Darlington Railway has become the world's first public steam-operated line. The business cases of light railway schemes which looked watertight on paper were, within a decade of their opening, rendered full of holes thanks to road transport's infinitely greater versatility and economy.

Furthermore, the loss of profits and the lack of government or local authority grant aid meant that there was no capacity for investment in repairs to cheaply-built basic infrastructure which in the longer term could not cope with the wear and tear from regular traffic.

Had Stephens' light rail businesses mushroomed 20 years sooner, in an age where rail transport still held the upper hand unchallenged, many of his lines would surely have thrived. As it was, their demise heralded the decline of country branch lines from the 1930s onwards, paving the way for the rail cutbacks of the Fifties and Sixties onwards.

However, the colonel would have been surprised to discover that, decades later, light railways operating to the provisions of the 1896 Act would become sizeable players in the UK tourism market.

Several observers have called Stephens, a legendary figure by virtue of his rich and varied selection of short rural independent lines, the forerunner of today's buoyant heritage railway sector, and if not its founding father, a major guiding light.

Yes, history shows that because of the advent of motor transport, his light railways may have come too late in the day despite his best intentions and those of his investors. Yet when you see the crowds flocking to today's 'preserved' railways and heritage venues, Colonel Stephens looks, albeit unwittingly, to have been light years ahead of his time.

certificate of Holman F Stephens. COLONEL STEPHENS SOCIETY

Installed on July 10, 2018, was the blue plaque in the booking hall at Tonbridge station which recalls Colonel Stephens' journey by train from the town where his light rail 'empire' had its offices in Salford Terrace. The Colonel Stephens Society's bid to have the plaque installed was supported by main line operator South Eastern Trains, Tonbridge & Malling Borough Council and the Kent & East Sussex Railway. COLONEL STEPHENS SOCIETY

One section of Colonel Stephens' light railway portfolio is still in passenger-carrying service today at part of the national network. A First Great Western DMYU is seen crossing the spectacular Calstock viaduct above the River Tamar on the Gunnislake branch, the truncated remains of Stephen's Callington branch which today forms part of the Tamar Valley Line. NICK LANSLEY*

Chapter 1

The Duke of Wellington's train and other locomotives being readied for departure from Liverpool on September 15, 1830, the official opening of the world's first inter-city line, the Liverpool & Manchester Railway.

Engineer George Stephenson, who was born in Street House in Wylam, nine miles west of Newcastle-upon-Tyne, on June 9, 1781, as the illiterate son of a labourer, went on to change the world. He showed a propensity for all things mechanical and paid for lessons to read and write once he had started work, going on to become a defining figure in the evolution of the steam locomotive.

TRANSPORT:
THE GREATEST LIBERATOR OF ALL, BUT...

The railway age of the 19th century used some of the finest fruits of the Industrial Revolution to shrink the globe forever, and deliver multiple benefits to populations worldwide. However, despite several decades of remarkable progress in the field of rapid transit, there were still swathes of the British countryside and its population which were missing out.

The 19th century may be considered the greatest era of change as far as the ordinary man and woman were concerned. For it was then that the door was opened to mobility on a scale never before imagined in the history of the human race.

The great innovation, of course, was the invention of the self-propelled railway locomotive, in its first incarnation as a portable steam engine.

Railways in themselves were by no means new; wooden-railed horse-drawn wagonways originated in Germany in the 16th century and such a system was once used by German miners at Caldbeck, Cumbria, maybe in the 1560s.

The York to London Royal Mail coach of 1820, as displayed in the Science Museum in London. It represented a technological improvement as it was built to stand the shocks of the bumpy roads of the day. It could manage the 200-mile journey at a speed of 8-10mph with the teams of horses changed around every 10 miles. ROBIN JONES

A freight-carrying tramway was built at Prescot, near Liverpool, maybe as early as 1594. Owned by Philip Layton, it carried coal from a pit near Prescot Hall to a transhipment point half a mile away. By the late 18th century, a patchwork of such local rail links operated by small private companies had developed to serve industrial needs. By 1671 railed roads were in use in Durham to make the carriage of coal more efficient, the first being the Tanfield Wagonway.

However, what of general travel for the population at large? The colossal advances made by the Romans in the field of roadbuilding had been lost in the wake of their departure from Britain aft

410AD, and a millennium later, in Tudor times, public highways were dirt tracks at best.

If you were lucky enough to own a horse or could afford to hire one, the roads could be used to travel across country, but a journey from London to Plymouth, for instance, would take a week. As far as most of the population was concerned, the average person would rarely travel beyond the hinterland of their home town and village. Many of those living inland might well spend their lives without ever seeing the sea.

Transport and communications began to develop in the 17th century. While at the start of the century the royal posts had carried only the king's correspondence, in 1635, as a moneymaking venture, Charles I allowed ordinary members of the public to pay his messengers to carry their letters too, and so began the royal mail.

By the mid-17th century, the cities and the bigger towns were linked by stagecoaches, though only the rich could afford to use them. Not only would they have offered markedly rough rides, without the addition of spring suspension on which to tackle the muddy potholed roads of the day, but there was always the risk of being stopped by highwaymen too.

The first turnpikes – roads which were improved using the revenue from tolls paid by users – were created as early as 1663. However, the concept really took off in the 18th century when groups of wealthy men formed turnpike trusts, give powers by Acts of Parliament to improve and maintain certain roads. Improved roads thereby became more commonplace, if by no means widespread. Travellers still had to pay to use them, with tolls being collected at houses built at gated intervals for the purpose.

The carriage of goods over the turnpikes using pack horses pushed up the prices by which they would eventually be sold. However, in 1759, the canal age began. The Duke of Bridgewater engaged engineer James Brindley to build an artificial waterway to carry coal by boat from his estate at Worsley to Manchester – and at a stroke halved the price of the black stuff. The success of the Bridgewater Canal led to many more canals being dug and rivers being made navigable by the installation of locks. This inland waterway network facilitated the Industrial Revolution by making the carriage of raw materials to foundries and factories

and the export of the finished product to market much cheaper.

However, for the average person, horses and carts were still the only form of transport available apart from foot.

The first passenger-carrying public railway was opened by the Swansea & Mumbles Railway at Oystermouth in 1807, using horse-drawn carriages on an existing tramway. However, it was still a small local affair and the concept would take many years to expand to a wider market. Yet world-shrinking transport technology had by been demonstrated in Wales three years earlier.

THE FIRST CARS

Austro-Hungarian army officer Nicolas-Joseph Cugnot demonstrated the world's first steam tractor in 1769. It has been described as the world's first self-propelled vehicle but it was a clumsy affair that came to grief by turning over in a Paris street.

Scottish inventor William Murdoch later experimented with steam traction. He was employed by the Birmingham firm of Boulton & Watt to work for them in Cornwall, erecting stationary steam engines for pumping water out of tin and copper mines. At his house at Redruth, which has been claimed to be the first domestic residence to be lit by gas, witnesses reported seeing a model steam carriage run around his living room in 1784. That is the first recorded example in the UK of a machine moving around completely under its own power.

Murdoch infamously ran a 19in-long three-wheeled steam carriage, possibly a model, one night along the lane leading to Redruth church. The machine ran loose at 8mph, terrifying the rector who believed that the devil was about to attack!

In 1797, Cornish mining engineer Richard Trevithick moved to the house next door, and Murdoch's son John later told of a visit by Trevithick and his engineer colleague Andrew Vivian to see a model engine three years earlier.

Trevithick increased the level of steam pressure in stationary engines so that he could make smaller versions – and realised that if they could power a machine or pump, it should be possible to adapt them to drive themselves. Such machines would at a stroke improve the conveyance of heavy mine engine components from the nearest port or harbour over the steep Cornish terrain, along with the carriage of the ores that had been extracted for export.

Trevithick and Vivian built a steam road carriage which, on Christmas Eve 1801, ascended Camborne Hill under its own power. Onlookers jumped aboard for a ride – effectively making it the world's first motor car! It was the definitive turning point – the greatest since the invention of the wheel itself.

It was to be the bridge link between the Industrial Revolution and the modern world. The big problem was that while Trevithick's self-propelled machine worked, it was far too heavy for the poor roads of the day. It was designed to run on the public highway but it immediately sank into the ground.

Undeterred, in 1802, Trevithick demonstrated his pioneer London Steam Carriage in the capital, offering trips from the city centre to Paddington and back, with up to eight guests on board.

It was the world's first motor bus, and the first official public running of a self-powered passenger vehicle. Yet as with Cugnot's vehicle, steering was the big problem and it ended up crashing into railings. The fault lay not with the machine, but again with the inadequate

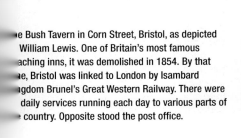

The Bush Tavern in Corn Street, Bristol, as depicted [by] William Lewis. One of Britain's most famous coaching inns, it was demolished in 1854. By that time, Bristol was linked to London by Isambard Kingdom Brunel's Great Western Railway. There were daily services running each day to various parts of the country. Opposite stood the post office.

"Good stabling and loose boxes": the Millstone pub in Stamford still prominently displays its selling point from the days when the yellowstone Lincolnshire town was a primary stopping point on the Great North Road. ROBIN JONES

roads of the day which could not support its weight.

A second carriage for London was built in 1803. Standing 13ft high, it proved too big and could not compete economically with a horse-drawn version.

Trevithick could not implement a road building programme just for the sake of his 'novelty' machines, so instead he turned to an existing concept – the horse-drawn tramway. This was world travel's big turning point.

EARLY STEAM RAILWAYS

In 1802, Trevithick built a railway locomotive for private use at Coalbrookdale ironworks in Shropshire, one of the celebrated cradles of the Industrial Revolution.

Two years later, he then built a locomotive which helped ironworks owner Samuel Homfray win a 500-guinea bet that a steam engine could haul 10 tons of iron over the horse-drawn tramroad linking Penydarren ironworks near Merthyr Tydfil to the Glamorganshire Canal.

The bet was won on February 21, 1804, after the world's first public demonstration of a steam locomotive was successfully carried out.

Trevithick's last locomotive, *Catch-Me-Who-Can*, briefly ran on a circle of track in 1808 near the site of the future Euston station.

Built along with its carriage at Hazeldine Foundry in Bridgnorth, Shropshire, by engineer John Urpeth Rastrick, it became the world's first steam passenger train, even though it was providing the function of little more than a circus novelty.

In a world where horses and carts still reigned supreme, Trevithick's road and rail vehicles were considered little more than that – novelties. A modern parallel might be drawn to the launch of computer pioneer Sir Clive Sinclair's Sinclair C5 small one-person battery electric velomobile, an "electrically assisted pedal cycle", in 1985. In a modern world increasingly and justifiably

The Trevithick Society's replica of Richard Trevithick and Andrew Vivian's steam road carriage which on Christmas Eve, 1801, ascended Camborne Hill under its own power. However, it would be steam-powered rail rather than road transport which would be the premier form of travel for the next century. The replica is pictured on April 28, 2018, during Camborne's annual Trevithick Day held in honour of the great Cornish mining engineer and inventor. ROBIN JONES

worried by climate change and concerned with the eradication of burning fossil fuels wherever possible, electric vehicles may well become the norm rather than the exception, but in its day the Sinclair C5 was quickly forgotten.

Discouraged by the initial lukewarm reaction to his locomotives, it appears that Trevithick had given up on the idea by 1810. They never made him a fortune: indeed, he died in poverty from pneumonia in Dartford's Bull Hotel on April 22, 1833.

However, it transpired that Trevithick's locomotives had by then already left an indelible mark in the minds of other inventors. History records, quite rightly, that the industrial North East became the "cradle of the railways". Yet it was a Cornish baby that had been placed into it.

In 1812, Matthew Murray's *Salamanca* appeared on the edge-railway Middleton Railway at Leeds. Not only was it the first steam locomotive to have two cylinders but it was also the first to be commercially successful.

The subject of first painting of a steam locomotive, *Salamanca* lasted for only six years before its boiler exploded, its driver said to have tampered with its safety valve. However, Murray's demonstration model of *Salamanca*, which preceded the building of the full-size version, is still with us today and was displayed in the National Railway Museum's award-winning Brass, Steel & Fire exhibition at York in 2019-20.

A chronic shortage of horses due to an overriding military need during the closing stages of the Napoleonic Wars led to despairing mine owners looking again at Trevithick's ideas in order to compensate for the shortage.

During 1813-14, engineer William Hedley, enginewright Jonathan Forster and blacksmith Timothy Hackworth built *Puffing Billy* for Wylam Colliery near Newcastle-upon-Tyne. The world's oldest surviving steam locomotive (which was used in service until 1862), it is now in the Science Museum in London. A year later, Killingworth Collieries enginewright George Stephenson improved on the design of *Puffing Billy* with his first locomotive *Blücher*, which was the first locomotive to use single-flanged wheels.

Cornish scientist and inventor Sir Goldsworthy Gurney was the first to run steam between London and Bristol, but by road, not rail, in July 1829, at an average speed of 14mph – two months before Stephenson's *Rocket* won the Rainhill Trials and paved the way for the future development of the steam railway locomotive. Gurney's steam carriage was not a commercial success: there was an apprehension on the part of the public to ride on a conveyance on top of a dangerous steam boiler, and so the age of the self-propelled road motor vehicle had to wait for several more decades.

These early steam locomotives had been designed purely for industrial use but on September 27, 1825, the Stockton & Darlington Railway, which was engineered by George Stephenson, opened. It was the first public railway in the world to use steam locomotives.

Far better was to come five years into the future, when on September 15, 1830, the Liverpool & Manchester Railway, also engineered by George Stephenson, became the world's first inter-city line and the first to have terminal stations and services as we know them today, setting the pattern for modern railways.

Furthermore, Stephenson's 0-2-2 *Rocket*, which he had designed purely for the Rainhill Trials, a contest to find

Built in Wales in 1981, here is the working replica of Trevithick's locomotive which helped ironworks owner Samuel Homfray win a 500-guinea bet that a steam locomotive would haul 10 tons of iron over the horse-drawn tramroad linking Penydarren ironworks near Merthyr Tydfil to the Glamorganshire Canal, on February 21, 1804, which saw the world's first public demonstration of a steam locomotive. The replica is seen in action during the Railfest 200 celebrations at the National Railway Museum in York in 2004. ROBIN JONES

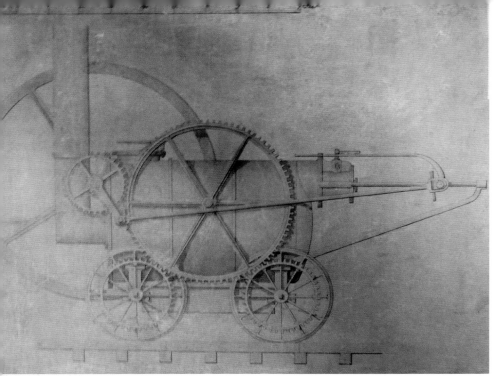

An original drawing for one of Richard Trevithick's railway locomotives held in the National Railway Museum archives at York. ROBIN JONES

This model of Matthew Murray's *Salamanca* of 1812 – the world's first commercially-successful steam locomotive – both pre-dated the full-size version and outlived it. Part of the Leeds Museums and Galleries collection, the model featured in the National Railway Museum's Brass, Steam & Fire exhibition, which won the 2020 Heritage Railway Association Interpretation Award, sponsored by Mortons Media Group Ltd/ *Heritage Railway* magazine. ROBIN JONES

the best from of traction for the illustrious new line, established the blueprint for future steam railway locomotive development.

The opening of the Liverpool & Manchester came 26 years after Trevithick's first public demonstration of a railway locomotive and illustrated just how slow the world had been to catch on to the concept. Its overnight success acted as a springboard for other steam-hauled railways big and small to be built across Britain, with the Grand Junction Railway linking it to Birmingham and the London & Birmingham Railway to the capital. The days of the stagecoach were gone for good.

While much of this transport revolution can rightly be attributed to the development of the steam railway locomotive from a passing curiosity to the premier form of transport in a quarter of a century, credit must also be given to the evolution of the rails themselves.

Those early wagonways built for use by horse-drawn carts were constructed using parallel wooden rails. The next stage of development occurred in 1793 when Benjamin Outram built a mile-long tramway with L-shaped cast iron rails.

In turn, Outram's railways were rendered obsolete when William Jessop began to manufacture cast iron rails without guiding ledges, with the wheels of the carts having flanges instead.

The big drawback here was the brittle nature of cast iron, with the rails tending to break easily. This had been evident as early as 1804 during the demonstration of Trevithick's locomotive at Pen-y-darren. So in 1820 John Birkenshaw introduced a method of

rolling wrought iron rails, which were used thereafter.

THE UK RAIL NETWORK TAKES SHAPE

Many of the first public railways were local affairs run by small companies. As the 1830s wore on, more and more schemes for public railways appeared, with several of the smaller companies amalgamating into larger and longer concerns, offering the ability to travel longer distances.

The social implications of the embryonic railway network were many, not least the creation of cheap access to the growing industrial centres for labour from the rural shires. Then there was the standardisation of time across the country: a train guard's watch would convey Greenwich Mean Time to every station called at, and the rest of the town and city would synchronise their timepieces from there.

The 1840s were by far the biggest decade for railway growth, characterised by the period known as Railway Mania. At the start of the decade there were still comparatively few railway lines in the UK, but lured by the prospect of rich dividends speculators clamoured to invest in all manner of schemes, some of which had clearly

The Trevithick 200 group's working replica of Trevithick's last locomotive, the passenger carriage-hauling *Catch-Me-Who-Can* of 1808. It was, like the original, built in Bridgnorth, and is pictured in the Severn Valley Railway's Bridgenorth yard in 2012. ROBIN JONES

not been properly costed with regards to their potential for the generation of traffic.

Railway Mania reached its height in 1846, when 272 Acts of Parliament were passed setting up new railway companies; their proposed routes totalled 9500 miles of new lines. However, about a third of these railways were, for various reasons, never built. Some of the companies collapsed, taking their investors' money with them, and others bought out by larger competitors.

It was in 1844 that the nationalisation of Britain's railway system was first mooted – not by any form of revolutionary socialist but one of the country's best-known Conservative and later Liberal politicians, William Ewart Gladstone.

When he was a Conservative Free Trader and president of the Board of Trade, he introduced into the House of Commons the bill for The Railway Regulation Act 1844 – or to give it its correct title "an Act to attach certain Conditions to the construction of future Railways authorised by any Act of the present or succeeding sessions of Parliament; and for other Purposes in relation to Railways". Here was the first piece of legislation that gave the British government the power to take over the nations railways, half a century before the Labour Party was born.

The primary purpose of the Act, passed under Sir Robert Peel's Conservative Government, was to force the railways, under threat of nationalisation, to reduce their charges in the interests of the whole body of capitalist manufacturers and traders.

The Act also enshrined in law the requirement to set affordable ticket prices for the poorer sections of society so they could travel to find work. Again, before the coming of the railways, it was said that most people never ventured more than 15 miles beyond their place of birth.

Furthermore, before the Act was passed, there were three or more classes of carriage, the lower or third class usually an open freight wagon. Gladstone's Act, as it was also colloquially known, stipulated that one train with provision for carrying third-class passengers should run on every line, every day, in each direction, stopping at every station, with a fare of no more than a penny a mile and up to 56lb of luggage per passenger carried free of charge. Also, it insisted that

The popular image of *Rocket* is more like how it appeared on the Liverpool & Manchester Railway. Over the past century several replicas have been built; this one, based at the National Railway Museum in York, was built by Mike Satow and Locomotive Enterprises in 1979 for the Rainhill 50th anniversary celebrations in 1980. ROBIN JONES

In the Opening of the Stockton and Darlington Railway, a watercolour painted in the 1880s by John Dobbin, crowds stand watching the inaugural train cross the Skerne Bridge in Darlington. Major celebrations are planned for the bicentenary of what was the world's first public steam-operated railway in 2025.

The winner of the Rainhill Trials of 1829, held to establish the optimum motive power for the Liverpool & Manchester Railway, the world's first inter-city line, Stephenson's *Rocket* became the blueprint for the future development of the steam locomotive and paved the way for mass rapid transit for the masses. After retirement from the Liverpool & Manchester, it ran on Lord Carlisle's Railway in Cumberland, modified for industrial service. In 1862 it was donated to the Patent Office Museum in London and was displayed in the Science Museum. In 2019, it was moved on long-term loan to the National Railway Museum in York. ROBIN JONES

third-class passengers should be protected from the weather and be provided with seats.

These so-called 'Parliamentary Trains' required train companies to provide at least one inexpensive and basic service for less affluent passengers each day on every railway route, and for the first time travel for the lower classes of the population over greater distances became affordable.

The Act's provision for nationalisation was never used, but the threat was sufficient to compel the railway companies to comply with the other measures contained in it.

By the end of the decade Britain's rail network, as it would by and large stand for more than another century, had taken shape, with most cities, towns and even larger villages having access to at least one rail connection and in many cases two or three.

THE 1896 LIGHT RAILWAYS ACT

During Victorian times and the early 20th century, the process of mergers, amalgamations and acquisitions continued, until the network was dominated by larger companies. However, from the mid-1870s, profits began to diminish across the UK rail industry, with companies trying to boost returns by pushing ahead with projects that were to prove uneconomic.

Profits and shareholders' dividends rather than social considerations remained at the forefront of the railway companies' reason for existence and the network had evolved to the point where larger centres of population were well served by rival routes. On the other hand, sparsely-populated rural shires often lack any rail communication whatsoever and still relied on horses and carts. Accordingly, despite the complexity of the network that had evolved, there will

still large swathes of the country that to a large extent remained in the pre-Stephenson era.

During the 1870s and 1880s, when agriculture was in severe depression, the only way for farmers to get their produce on to the national market was by rail, but lines were very expensive to build.

Almost a century before Dr Beeching, rural areas faced losing their rail links with the outside world, and entrepreneurs and politicians were desperate to find a solution which was based on the steam locomotive but was cheap to build and operate.

The government looked at ways by which railways could be built to serve such rural areas, especially to facilitate the transport of goods.

The response was the Light Railways Act 1896, which made the building of railways to serve rural 'outbacks' less economically daunting. This swept away

The London & North Western Railway 'Bloomer' 2-2-2s appeared in 1851 and hauled trains between London and Birmingham at up to 70mph in just two hours, again boosting rail transport's role as a 'liberator' which allowed the public to reach destinations at speeds that could not have been imagined even two decades earlier.

These powerful express engines were developed in 1851 from a design by LNWR Southern Division locomotive superintendent James McConnell's predecessor Edward Bury, in collaboration with Charles Beyer, the German engineer who went on to found Beyer Peacock & Co in Manchester. They were built at the railway's Wolverton Works and were considered ahead of their time, with high 120psi boiler pressure, hopper grates for removing ash and clinker and experimental fireboxes designed to run on coal not coke.

The class locomotive took its nickname campaigning American feminist Amelia Bloomer. Anything novel or striking was likely to be labelled as a 'Bloomer.' Her reforms in dress which shocked contemporary Victorian society revealed ladies' legs – the locomotive showed its 'naked' driving wheels and the lower part of its 'anatomy'!

While no 'Bloomer' has survived, Tyseley Locomotive Works has been building a working replica and plans to create a matching rake of carriages. Numbered 670 after the works' address in Warwick Road, Tyseley, Birmingham, the new 'Bloomer' is seen on display at the Warley Model Railway Exhibition at the National Exhibition Centre near Birmingham. PAUL BICKERDYKE

The primary emphasis on the development of the UK railway network was to connect large centres of population and industry often in as short a time as possible, the incentive being profits and rich dividends for railway company shareholders.

When Patrick Stirling was appointed to the Great Northern Railway as Locomotive Superintendent in 1866, he had speed as his aim. The most famous of his locomotives were the Stirling Singles, 4-2-2s with distinctive 8ft 1in driving wheels and domeless boilers, nicknamed 'eight footers', and appearing in 1870, became distinctive images of Victorian railway technology at its finest… and fastest, as they headed high-speed expresses between York and London.

These locomotives could haul 275-ton trains at an average of 50mph and lighter trains at 85mph. Yes, Victorian technology was shrinking the country, but there were still substantial rural areas that were missing out on the railway age.

The surviving Stirling Single, No. 1, part of the National Collection, is seen at the head of a train of teak coaches at the Doncaster Works open day in 2003.
ROBIN JONES

restrictions and supplemented local finance with central government funds to create 'no-frills' lines which avoided hills whenever possible, incorporated sharp curves, steep gradients and basic stations, and utilised light rails and locomotives.

The theory was that such railways would be built to accommodate the anticipated agricultural traffic as well as passengers, and if successful after the first few years they would be upgraded. If not, the financial loss was minimal.

Before this legislation came into being, each new railway line built in the country required a specific act of parliament to be obtained by the company that sought to build it. That in itself added greatly to the expense and time needed to construct new railways.

The 1896 act spelled out a new 'sub class' of railways which did not needs specific legislation to build. Companies could simply plan a line under the provisions of the act, proceed to obtain a Light Railway Order, and then construct and operate it.

By reducing the legal costs and allowing new railways to be built quickly without too much fuss, the government hoped to encourage the big companies to build the new breed light railways in areas of low population and industry that up to now had been of little interest to them.

This new generation of lines, coming seven decades after the opening of the watershed Stockton & Darlington Railway, were not just 'light railways' but 'railways lite', built on the cheap without requirements that were mandatory on existing routes.

The 1896 Act in many ways followed in the wake of the Regulation of Railways Act 1868 which had permitted the construction of light railways subject to "… such conditions and regulations as the Board of Trade may from time to time impose or make". These conditions specified a maximum permitted axle weight and stated that "…the regulations respecting the speed of trains shall not authorize a rate of speed exceeding at any time 25mph".

That speed limit is often erroneously credited to the 1896 Act, but was inherited from the earlier legislation. It applies to today's heritage railways, and famously was quoted by the railway inspector in the concluding scenes of the 1953 Ealing comedy The Titfield Thunderbolt, when he approved the blundering Mallingford townfolk's bid to take over their closed branch line purely because their ancient museum piece locomotive had not broken the magic 25mph limit.

The 1896 Act bestowed powers on the Light Railway Commissioners to include "provisions for the safety of the public… as they think necessary for the proper construction and working of the railway" in any Light Railway Order granted under the legislation. These provisions could limit vehicle axle weights and speeds – yes, the maximum speed of 25mph. Such limits were deemed essential when lightly-laid track and relatively modest bridges were used in order to keep costs down.

Light Railway Orders could also exempt light railways from some of the requirements of a normal railway – level crossings did not have to be protected by gates, but only by cattle grids, saving the cost of both the gates and a keeper to operate them.

Many of the lines built under the provisions of the 1896 Act were very basic, with little or no signalling, with many of them operating under the 'one engine in steam' principle.

Several municipal and company-owned street tramways were built or extended by the 1896 Act, in preference to the more complicated Tramways Act 1870. The 1896 Act provided for a 75% savings on rates payable as compared to a tramway.

LAST BLASTS OF THE BIG RAILWAY BUILDERS

The 1896 Light Railway Act came as the great age of railway building was approaching its end, although it many respects id did not anticipate that final curtain call.

The Great Central Railway's London Extension was the last complete trunk railway to be built in Britain until section one of High Speed 1, the Channel Tunnel Rail Link, opened in 2003.

The Manchester, Sheffield & Lincolnshire Railway obtained Parliamentary approval in 1893 for the 92-mile extension and on August 1, 1897, duly changed its name. The extension opened for coal traffic on July 25, 1898, passenger traffic on March 15, 1899 and for general goods traffic on April 11, 1899. Designed for high-speed running throughout, it was also one of the shortest-lived inter-city routes, closing in stages between 1966-69.

Shortly afterwards, the Great Western Railway created a new through main line route from the West Midlands to South Wales and the West of England by taking over in 1900 the Birmingham, North Warwickshire and Stratford Railway, which had received royal assent in August 1894 but failed to raise the necessary funds to build the line. The GWR incorporated the line into its own scheme to build a new Birmingham to Cheltenham via Stratford main line, avoiding the Midland Railway's notorious Lickey Incline. The line was opened to goods traffic on December 9, 1907, and to passengers on July 1, 1908.

Through services to Gloucester were withdrawn in 1968, and passenger services south of Stratford ceased altogether on May 5, 1969, when the service to Honeybourne, Evesham and Worcester Foregate Street was withdrawn. However the line remained open for freight until 1976, when a serious freight train derailment at Winchcombe led to British Rail closing the route line and leaving Stratford as its southern terminus. Today, the North Warwickshire

Line from Birmingham is a busy and essential commuter route.

That is not to say that the big railway companies stopped building new lines or improving existing ones after those dates, but the great age of railway building was visibly over.

The 1896 Light Railways Act did not succeed in penetrating anywhere near all of Britain's rural areas that had been ignored and left untouched by railway promoters – Hartland in north Devon has often been said to be the largest rural community in England that found itself unserved by rail (although there had been plans to link it to Bideford drawn up in the 1860s), and the GWR's branch to Kingsbridge on the other side of the country was never extended further south to the fishing port of Salcombe, despite some earthworks taking shape.

HAIL THE NEW KING

Motor road transport has one distinct advantage over railways – that it is not physically restricted to travelling on a fixed route.

A lorry can offer a door-to-door service while cutting out the 'middle man' of the railway and its usually higher cost, while for the general public, the car set out on the road to become the great universal liberator, allowing the owner to drive from anywhere to anywhere, without being restricted to the limitations of a railway route or an inconvenient train timetable.

Cars came into use on British roads during the early 1890s, but the first vehicles were imported from abroad. In 1885, Karl Benz developed a petrol or gasoline-powered automobile, which is also considered to be the first 'production' vehicle as Benz made several identical examples. It was powered by a single cylinder four-stroke engine.

Frederick William Bremer built Britain's first car with an internal combustion engine. Born in 1872, the son of a German immigrant, he was an electrician, engineer and bicycle maker who lived in Walthamstow and assembled his car in a workshop behind the family's home on Connaught Road. He built it for personal pleasure rather than commercial profit and first drove it in 1892, with an assistant holding a red flag walking in front of it to comply with the laws of the day.

Following, extensive restoration, Bremer's vehicle completed the veteran car race from London to Brighton in the 1960s in seven hours and 55 minutes. The car itself is now displayed at Vestry House Museum in Walthamstow.

It has been said that the roots of the British motor industry can be traced back to the 1880s when London consulting engineer Frederick Simms became friends with German engineer, industrial

designer and industrialist Gottlieb Daimler who patented a successful design for a high-speed petrol engine in 1885. Simms bought the UK rights to Daimler's engine and from 1891 sold launches using these German motors from Eel Pie Island in the River Thames. June 1895 saw Simms and his friend Evelyn import a Daimler-engined Panhard & Levassor to England and the following month it completed the first British long-distance motor car journey, from Southampton to Malvern.

Simms planned to build Daimler motors and cars in the UK, but his company and its licences were taken over by London company promoter H J Lawson who, in January 1896, formed The Daimler Motor Syndicate Limited. The firm then bought a disused cotton mill in Coventry where, some claim, Britain's first production car was made.

Also in 1896, John Henry Knight of Farnham, Surrey, built a four-wheeled petrol-engined car while George and Frederick Lanchester constructed a similar vehicle in Birmingham.

In 1904, Henry Royce outshopped his first car, a two-cylinder model, and later that year met aviator C S Rolls who agreed to sell it in his London showroom. They pair become Rolls-Royce Limited in 1906.

In 1901, five years after the passing of the Light Railways Act, trains and not cars were still the preferred premier form of transport for the population at large, but the writing began to appear on the wall. Then, cars were still very much a luxury commodity, mainly used for pleasure rather than business, but were welcomed by professionals such as doctors who had to travel on a daily basis. By the end of 1904, there were 23,000 cars on Britain's road and more than 100,000 by 1910.

Early attempts to produce cars in the UK proved short-lived because of the lack of capital investment. Most of the pioneering car producers, many of them from the bicycle industry, got off to a shaky start. Of the 200 British car companies that had been launched up before 1913, only about 100 of them were still running by that time. In 1910, UK production was around 14,000 cars.

However, by 1908, cheaper Fords had begun to arrive from the USA. In 1913, the Ford Model T, then five years old, became the first automobile to be mass-produced on a moving assembly line. Ford built a new factory in Manchester that year and overnight became the leading UK producer, with 7310 cars turned out in the first year alone. The Model T contributed greatly to the transformation of the motor car from a rich man's toy into an affordable means of transport for ordinary people.

The wheel had turned full circle again.

The year before the First World War broke out, Wolseley was producing

Laying the foundations for the Great Central Railway's Marylebone station in the mid-1890s. It would be the terminus of the last complete trunk railway to be built in the steam age. ILLUSTRATED LONDON NEWS

Much has been made about the sizeable north Devon village of Hartland being the furthest away from a railway station in England, the nearest being Bude and Bideford, both of which were closed under the Beeching Axe of the 1960s. Plans to build a railway to Hartland never materialised, and 'ts Fore Street is pictured in the first half of the 20th century. ROBIN JONES COLLECTION

The sizeable South Devon harbour town of Salcombe, today long renowned as a well-to-do yachtman's paradise, missed out on the railway age. A Kingsbridge and Salcombe Railway scheme was authorised by Parliament on July 29, 1864, but it failed to attract sufficient investment after the GWR took over the scheme. A branch was built only as far as Kingsbridge, opening on December 19, 1893. A proposed extension to Salcombe was never completed. The 1896 Light Railways Act aimed to facilitate the building of country railways 'on the cheap' to serve such areas that had been left unconnected to the national rail network, but history records it was to be 'too little too late' as the motor transport revolution was beginning. ROBIN JONES

3000 cars, Humber, which had made cars in Coventry since 1898, turned out 2500, Rover 1800, also in Coventry, and Sunbeam 1700. Altogether in 1913, around 16,000 cars were produced in Britain, although production all but halted during the ensuing war years.

Furthermore, to give a fuller account of how developments in transport technology changed the lives of ordinary people forever by facilitating greater mobility, the emergence of the bicycle should not be overlooked.

The 1890s saw a phenomenal growth in the popularity of cycling, with around 50,000 people in Britain employed in bicycle manufacturing. The bicycle provided the ordinary man and woman with an affordable (and eco-friendly into the bargain) means of private transport for the first time in history. The bicycle was an affordable machine even then and they were mainly used by younger people and the less well-off sections of the community.

The modern diamond-pattern bicycle frame, with roller-chain drive and pneumatic tyres, was firmly established in 1893. The next phase of its development came with the patenting of Sturmey-Archer gears in 1901 and 1906.

THE BUS REVOLUTION STARTED BY RAILWAYS

When it became clear during the early years of the 20th century that motor road vehicles would shape the future of transport, the GWR looked at providing bus services both as a feeder to its train services and as a cheaper alternative to building new branch lines in sparsely-populated rural areas as facilitated by the 1896 Act. Indeed, the GWR ran the first bus services successfully operated by a UK railway.

When looking at serving the Lizard peninsula in Cornwall, the GWR baulked

A motor car like this one built by pre-eminent French manufacturers Panhard & Levassor won the world's first motor race in 1895. Early motor car manufacturers used road races to enhance their reputation. The same year, motoring pioneer and MP Evelyn Ellis brought this vehicle, now displayed in London's Science Museum, to the UK as the country's first imported car. He used it to mount a successful challenge to legislation hampering both the development of the motor car in the UK and their use in the country, paving the way for the greatest challenge to rail travel. This was happening just as the 1896 Light Railways Act was passed in a bid to enable railways to access rural parts of the country which the bigger companies had hitherto not considered worth reaching. ROBIN JONES

A 1909 Ford Model T, the car which made motoring accessible and affordable in the UK at a time when railways still reigned supreme.

at the idea of spending £85,000 on extending the Helston branch by building a light railway to serve Britain's southernmost village, remote Lizard Town, and decided to try motor buses instead.

Two vehicles that had been used temporarily by the Lynton & Barnstaple Railway were acquired and the service was launched on August 17, 1903. It proved so popular and profitable that other routes were soon established, first locally to Mullion, Ruan Minor and Porthleven, and then further afield at Penzance.

A bus route from Slough station to Beaconsfield was launched on March 1, 1904, followed by routes to Windsor on July 18 that year. Indeed, the first GWR double deckers appeared on the Slough-Windsor service in 1904 onwards. A route from Wolverhampton

to Bridgnorth was briefly operated from November 7, 1904, using steam buses, with motor buses replacing them the following year.

The final bus services operated by the GWR began in the Weymouth area in 1935, jointly run with the London & South Western Railway, and were transferred to Southern National on January 1, 1934.

By the end of 1904, 36 buses were in GWR operation, and when the Great Western Railway (Road Transport) Act was passed in 1928, the GWR boasted the biggest railway bus fleet. This act paved the way for the services to be transferred

The Marble Arch.

Catching on in the capital: motor transport around Marble Arch in the early 1900s.

Around the same time that the motor car industry was beginning to lay down its first roots, bicycles had caught the public imagination and by 1895, millions were said to be using them on a daily basis, thereby improving transport for all. That year, bicycles were allowed into London's Hyde Park during permitted hours for the first time, with horses all but having vanished.

to bus companies, although the railway was to be a shareholder in these operations. So on January 1, 1929, the GWR routes in Devon and Cornwall transferred to the new Western National Omnibus Company, 50% owned by the railway and the other half by the National Omnibus and Transport Company. That year the GWR acquired 30% of the shares in the Devon General Omnibus and Touring Company.

An early GWR single decker. The GWR broke new ground with the successful running of regular bus services. GWT COLLECTION

As with the other major companies, the GWR operated an extensive fleet of road vehicles to supplement its rail services. Like the buses, the lorries and vans by and large had bodies built at Swindon, with the chassis bought in from outside manufacturers such as Mills-Daimler, Thornycroft and AEC.

Again, who would risk capital by building a railway on the cheap to serve rural

communities which would by themselves probably never make it pay?

While its architects and backers had clearly meant well, the 1896 Light Railways Act was never a great success. Coming late in the day, many of its products were among the first victims of the next phase of transport evolution – the motor cars, buses and lorries which took away passengers and goods traffic.

As with nearly all things political, both then or now, it was too late. The costs of building railways, even 'cheap' railways, could still not be kept low enough. Local financing was not available, central grants were inadequate, and the main line railway companies were not interested.

In 1898, two years after the passing of the Act, there were 88 applications to build light railways, in what might be seen as a 'rural Railway Mania' in miniature. By 1914 this number had plummeted to two, and the legislation was widely regarded as having failed. By the 1920s, road transport had killed off the majority of the little railways that it spawned, although some survived longer thanks to clever management and tight financial control.

In this narrow field, one man emerged head and shoulders about the rest. He became the single most important figure associated with the light railway boom: Colonel Holman Frederick Stephens.

GWR bus AF84 working a service from Helston to the Lizard in 1904.

Guy FBB 32 YF714, a 1927-built survivor from the GWR Cornish bus fleet which may have been used on services to Lizard Town. When the GWR fleet became part of Western National, YF714 retained its fleet number, 1268, but was repainted from GWR livery into the new corporate colours of green with a cream band. Later withdrawn from service, it was converted into a caravan at Perranporth and later a workshop, yet all of its mechanical components survived. Bought by bus enthusiast Robin Jenkinson for £60 in 1972, it was acquired by Colin and Helen Billington, and its restoration was completed at Maidenhead. It is seen in the car park of Slough station at the Thames Valley and Great Western Omnibus Trust's heritage weekend on Sunday, October 19, 2014. Competition from buses killed off many of the rural lines built under the 1896 Light Railways Act but also many of the routes closed on the recommendation of British Railways chairman Dr Richard Beeching in the 1960s. MARTIN49*

Chapter 2

Future light railway pioneer Holman Fred Stephens aged 18. He had reached the height of 6ft 2in by the age of 15. CSRM

The preserved signalbox at Hawkhurst. CLIVE WARNEFORD*

BEGINNINGS OF AN EMPIRE

Unlike those other great pioneers Richard Trevithick, George Stephenson and Isambard Kingdom Brunel, Colonel Holman Fred Stephens emerged at the end of the age of railway building. He was the man of the moment at the great cusp between the railway age and the dawn of the era of road motor transport. He became synonymous with light railways, of which be built or managed no fewer than 16, in what was the final valiant attempt to bring the benefits of the railways to rural communities that had missed out on them.

Holman Fred Stephens was the son of Pre-Raphaelite artist Frederic George Stephens and his wife the artist Rebecca Clara (née Dalton), born in the family home at 10 Hammersmith Terrace, Hammersmith, west London, on Saturday, October 31, 1868.

He was named after his father's friend and former tutor, the painter William Holman Hunt, one of the founders of the Pre-Raphaelite Brotherhood (who had changed his surname from Hobman Hunt to Holman Hunt when he discovered that a clerk had misspelled the name after his baptism). Holman Hunt became the godfather to young Holman although he later fell out with the boy's father, who at one stage became Keeper of Prints and Drawings at the British

Museum, while writing extensively about art history.

Holman was also a great nephew of the naturalist, explorer and biologist Charles Darwin. The poet Alfred Lord Tennyson once said he was "the most beautiful boy I have ever seen".

One of his earliest presents from his father was a working model of a railway engine, which survives to this day.

Portrait of Clare Stephens, the mother of Holman Fred Stephens, a watercolour by his father Frederic George Stephens, c.1865. NATIONAL GALLERY OF CANADA

An 1853 pencil drawing of Holman Fred Stephens' father, British art critic Frederic George Stephens, by John Everett Millais.

Frederic had undertaken some railway surveying work as a student in the 1840s. Young Holman attended Frederic's old school, University College, and in the summer of 1883, he visited Vitre in France to stay with the Rossignol family and while there he not only studied the French railway system to compare it with that of the UK, but also the local infantry regiment.

August 1886 saw him stay with a Professor Kienitz and his family at Karlsruhe in Germany and again he studied both railways and the local military. That year he began making inquiries about joining a military unit as a volunteer. He considered signing up for the School of Musketry at Hythe and also the Middlesex Yeomanry in London, but settled on joining the University College army cadet force.

Young Stephens matriculated in 1887, but stayed on for a further year at the college, studying under Sir Alexander Kennedy who had established a laboratory there to support his engineering students.

Frederic then arranged with John Bell, general manager of the Metropolitan Railway, for his son to become an apprentice at Neasden Works in 1881. He worked under locomotive superintendent John Hanbury, who himself had served an apprenticeship under the Midland Railway's Chief Mechanical Engineer Matthew Kirtley at Derby. Stephens now clamoured for experience in civils work, which he felt was his true forte.

Hanbury pointed him in the direction of consulting engineer of 20 years' experience Edward Parke Seaton, who was carrying out extensive alterations at Baker Street and Portland Road stations for the Metropolitan.

Stephens met Seaton and may well have impressed him with his family' acquaintance with Sir Edward Watkin, chairman of both the South Eastern Railway and the Metropolitan, who later became responsible for the construction of the Great Central's main line, Britain's last trunk route of the steam age, as mentioned in Chapter 1. In any event, Seaton took on the 22-years-old Stephens as resident engineer for the Cranbrook & Paddock Wood Railway.

STEPHENS' FIRST RAILWAY PROJECT

The construction between 1842 and 1853 of the Ashford to Hastings Line, the Tonbridge to Hastings line and South Eastern Main Line between Redhill and Folkestone left a triangle of land within the Kentish High Weald, a heavily wooded and agricultural area which comprised many small villages and hamlets, devoid of rail communication.

The three largest settlements in this area were Cranbrook, the former heart of the defunct Wealden cloth industry, Hawkhurst and Tenterden. There were no large landowners or wealthy industrialists to promote a branch line, while the local South Eastern Railway (SER) chose to wait until local enterprise had funded the route's construction.

The nominally-independent (of the SER) Weald of Kent Railway obtained an Act of Parliament in 1864 to build a

Aged just 22, Holman Fred Stephens proudly stands next to the opening train at Hope Mill (late Goudhurst) station on the Cranbrook & Paddock Wood Railway or Hawkhurst branch on October 1, 1892. CSRM

Holman Fred Stephens (second from left) with a theodolite. CSRM

Cudworth 2-4-0 No.112 at Goudhurst station with coach and posing figures on September 12, 1893.

nine-mile line from Paddock Wood to Cranbrook under the auspices of the London, Chatham & Dover Railway. However, because the latter was declared bankrupt in 1866, the scheme stalled until 1877 when the independent Cranbrook & Paddock Wood Railway was incorporated to build a similar line to be worked by the SER.

The powers were allowed to lapse following struggles to raise the necessary finance and further Acts had to be obtained in 1882, 1887 and 1892 before the line was finally completed, with financial backing from the SER. The 1882 Act also authorised a two-mile extension from Cranbrook to Hawkhurst.

Stephens was officially credited with assisting in the design of 20 small bridges, two short tunnels and six stations. He also claimed to have designed 13 houses along the route. However, Stephens' main role was to ensure that the contractor, J T Firbank, undertook the work efficiently and to scheduled.

While engaged on the project, Stephens lived at Cranbrook and met William Henry Austen, who would become his long-time associate (and as we will see, his eventual successor).

Stephens' input into the scheme was mentioned favourably by company chairman Lord Medway at the official launch of the line on October 1, 1892, when it opened from Paddock Wood to Goudhurst. It was extended from Goudhurst to Hawkhurst on September 4, 1893, but plans to extend it to Rye, making it a through route from London to the south coast, never materialised. Lord Medway's younger brother Alfred Erskine Gathorne-Hardy served as head of the Light Railway Commissioners until he died in 1918.

The South Eastern & Chatham Railway (SECR) absorbed the Cranbrook & Paddock Wood Railway in 1900, and in turn became part of the Southern Railway at the Grouping of 1923.

On July 6, 1950, the Queen Mother travelled the line as far as Cranbrook

when she visited the National Sanatorium at Benenden. The five-coach Royal Train was pulled by Maunsell E1 class 4-4-0 No. 31067. During the early 1950s, more than 4000 hop-pickers and around 23,000 visitors travelled over the branch in 56 'hopper specials' – extra services laid on during the late August-early October hop season. During the busiest period, up to six trains per day ran through to the branch from London. This activity earned the branch the nickname of 'The Hop Pickers Line'.

The Hawkhurst branch closed two years before the Beeching report was published. The inconvenient siting of stations and the decline in hop-picking in the area all contributed to diminishing returns on the line by the late 1950s. Hop pickers' specials aside, the line proved unpopular with commuters due to the poor connections to and from London. Indeed, in later years, only the line's expanding pot plant traffic justified its continuing existence.

Elisabeth Beresford, who acquired fame as the creator of the Wombles, wrote a children's book Danger on the Old Pull'n Push based on the Hawkhurst branch. It was televised by Rediffusion for ITV in two six-part series – The Old Pull'n Push and Return of the Old Pull'n Push – which were filmed on the line and shown in 1960-61.

Closure notices were posted in March 1961 and the last day of regular services was Saturday, June 10, 1961 when a pair of SECR C class 0-6-0s replaced the usual H class tank engines. On the last 5pm train from Hawkhurst every seat was taken by locals and railway enthusiasts. The last public train of all ran the next day, hauled by Class O1 0-6-0 No. 31065 piloting C class No. 31592, as part of a railtour organised by the Locomotive Club of Great Britain.

The special, 'The South Eastern Limited,' ran over the line as part of its Farewell to Steam tour and later that day it also navigated the surviving section of the Kent & East Sussex Railway from Robertsbridge to Tenterden. Both locomotives are today part of the Bluebell Railway's collection.

The track of the Hawkhurst branch was lifted in 1964. However, the line would not be allowed to pass forgotten into history.

In September 2008, representatives from Hawkhurst, Goudhurst, Horsmonden and Paddock Wood parish councils met to discuss the possibility of converting all or part of the former line into a trail which could be used by cyclists and walkers. The meeting led to the formation of the Hop Pickers Line Heritage Group.

In 2014, estimates were obtained for turning the trackbed into a trail as planned, but the necessary funding was not forthcoming. As a result, in partnership with Tunbridge Wells

The midway station of Goudhurst on the Cranbrook & Paddock Wood Railway as seen in Edwardian times. It was originally known as Hope Mill for Goudhurst & Lamberhurst and was the terminus of the line for just over 11 months, until the extension to Hawkhurst was opened on September 4, 1893. Stephens adopted the style of station buildings on the line for future use on his railways. The station featured in the 1953 children's film Adventures in the Hopfields.

Horsmonden station on the Cranbrook & Paddock Wood Railway in 1913, with oast houses, a trademark feature of the Wealden locality, in the background. The station has been converted to a private garage trading as the Old Station Garage, with the old stationmaster's house in use as a private dwelling.

Wainwright H Class 0-4-4T No.31500 at Horsmonden in British Railways days. CSRM

notice proclaiming the last train on the Hawkhurst anch, on June 10, 1961. CSRM

interpretation scheme for the Hop Pickers Line project, joined with Southeastern Railway managers at Paddock Wood station for the formal opening of the first information panel for the Hop Pickers Line project. Researched and produced by designer Martyn Hey, the panels provide a map showing the 11-mile route of the original line.

In formally opening the panels and cutting a special celebration cake, Councillor Elizabeth Thomas, chairman of Paddock Wood Town Council, spoke of Paddock Wood's proud railway heritage, congratulating all those involved in providing a wealth of interesting information and social history to be appreciated by both residents and visitors to this scenic part of the Garden of England that had been opened up by Holman Stephens.

DOORS OPENING AFTER CRANBROOK

The building of the Cranbrook & Paddock Wood Railway was an invaluable learning experience for Stephens. After it opened, he remained on the line for its maintenance period, making fresh contacts including Sir Myles Fenton, general manager of the SER, who promised to make him supervisor of the proposed extension of the Hawkhurst line to Appledore. However, that scheme did not go ahead.

Stephens was then engaged on surveying the proposed Tenterden Railway, a nearby scheme which also failed to take off. However, Seaton had been sufficiently impressed by Stephens that he proposed his application for associate membership of the Institution of Civil Engineers. Others proposed included William Wainwright, father of the subsequent SECR locomotive, carriage and wagon superintendent Harry Wainwright, and James Stirling, locomotive superintendent of the Glasgow & South Western Railway and later the SER. Stephens attained the associate membership in 1894, and it allowed him to design and build railways in his own right.

The following year, as a civil engineer he became involved with the Cranbook & District Water Company, and sought flood prevention work in Tonbridge to broaden his experience beyond railways. His advice was sought by the promoters of a light railway to serve collieries in the Clydach Valley, a scheme which developed into the Gower Light Railway. It was designed to link Port Eynon to the existing Swansea & Mumbles railway and was authorised by the Board of Trade on October 4, 1898.

One of the aims of the scheme was to provide greater accessibility to the Gower Peninsula for the people of Swansea and also holidaymakers. It failed to receive financial backing though, and so never got off the ground.

Stephens was next given a brief to design and supervise the Rye & Camber

Borough Council, the group changed its focus to commissioning an archaeological report of the line, which was completed in January 2016 by the AOC Archaeological Group. This report can be referred to when applying for local listings of the line's structures and features, thereby further helping to conserve the line's unique heritage for future generations.

The group then undertook an innovative waymarking interpretation scheme, featuring finger posts, marker posts and information panels for use in places where the line is still accessible or visible. This initiative was launched in November 2016, in conjunction with the developers of a solar farm at Paddock Wood.

On July 4, 2017, representatives of local communities, together with local authority partners in the new

The north end of Badgers Oak Tunnel on the Hawkhurst branch as seen in June 2013. TIM SCOLE

Tramway, which would be his second railway.

THE RYE & CAMBER TRAMWAY: AN 'INSTANT RAILWAY'

The modest 1¾-mile Rye & Camber Tramway line was built between January and July 1895 to 3ft gauge, unusual among railways on the UK mainland (the Southwold Railway is the most famous example), but commonplace in Ireland and the Isle of Man.

Thanks to the raw enthusiasm of the young Stephens, it was built within 14 weeks of the establishment of the Rye & Camber Tramways Company Ltd and was publicly opened on July 13, 1895. Running entirely on private land, its purpose was to carry golfers from Rye station to Rye Golf Club, and also beachgoers to the nearby sand dunes. It was extended by half a mile to Camber Sands in 1908.

It eventually had three stations – Rye, Golf Links and Camber Sands, which in 1938 was diverted to a more accessible site with a tea hut opening and which was used for only a few months before the Second World War broke out. For the station buildings, as consulting engineer Stephens adopted the style of the Cranbrook & Paddock Wood Railway, and he engaged the builder of that line's stations, Mancktelow Brothers of Horsmonden to build them. The firm also laid the track.

The little line was successful in its first years, but – in a story that we will see repeated time and again over the coming chapters – increasing competition from automobile and bus transport eventually caused its gradual economic decline. In its early years, the golf club subsidised winter running, but it ended its subsidy in 1925, after which the tramway ran only in the summer months, taking visitors to the beach.

The tramway had two small Bagnall 2-4-0Ts, *Camber* (built in 1895) and *Victoria* (1897), but in 1924 a small

Camber at the head of both Rye & Camber Tramway carriages at Rye station. CSRM

Bagnall 2-4-0T *Camber* with a single-coach train in the tramway's early years. CSRM

Heading for the beach in the Thirties. CSRM

This petrol locomotive pictured at the head of a train at Camber Sands became the mainstay of services after it arrived on the tramway in 1924, and reflected Stephens' other moves toward internal combustion power elsewhere. CSRM

A two-coach train passes Golf View house at Camber. CSRM

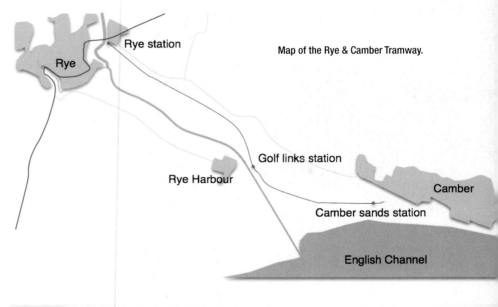

Map of the Rye & Camber Tramway.

four-wheeled First World War trench railways Simplex-type petrol locomotive built (or converted from an earlier locomotive) by the Kent Construction Company was acquired and was used almost exclusively on services.

Stephens was pleased. He had hoped to work the tramway from the outset with an internal combustion-powered tramcar, being mindful of the rapid changes taking place in the transport technology of the day, but in this thinking he was too far ahead of his time.

There were two enclosed carriages, one built by Bagnall and the other by the Rother Iron Works of Rye. Two four-wheel wagons were also fitted with seats for passengers and several locally-built four-wheel wagons were used to convey sand from the beach for local builders. Several temporary sidings were constructed at the Camber end for this purpose, where the dug-out dunes can still

Golf Links station on the 3ft gauge Rye & Camber Tramway today. The rails are still embedded in the concrete and building has since had the canopy enclosed. ROBIN WEBSTER*

The end is nigh at Rye: nature reclaims the tramway in its final days. CSRM

be seen. Rye-based novelist, biographer, memoirist, archaeologist and short story writer Edward Benson (July 24, 1867 – February 29, 1940) featured the tramway in several of his novels.

Passenger services ended on Sunday, September 4, 1939, the day after Britain declared war on Germany. The army occupied the station buildings on October 31, 1940, as anti-aircraft installations and minefields appeared around Camber. The military even considered a plan to extend the 15in gauge Romney, Hythe & Dymchurch Railway to Rye via the tramway's trackbed for further defensive purposes, but when the threat of Nazi invasion from the English Channel lessened, such ideas took a permanent back seat.

December 12, 1942, saw the Royal Navy move in and use the tramway to carry out improvements to the east of Rye Harbour. They would remain there until May 18, 1945. In the meantime, the

tramway played a part in the PLUTO (Pipe Line Under The Ocean, or originally Pipe-Line Underwater Transportation of Oil) project. PLUTO was a joint operation by British engineers, oil companies, and the British Armed Forces to lay oil pipelines beneath the English Channel in support of Operation Overlord, the Allied invasion of Normandy in June 1944. For this purpose, a special siding leading to a new pier near Golf Links Station was constructed by Canadian troops.

Sadly, the little line was so badly run down by the end of the war that it was deemed irrecoverable. By September that year, dismantling had begun and the line was sold for scrap in 1947. Today, Golf Links station building survives virtually intact and some track is embedded in concrete near the station as the trackbed was used as a roadway during wartime. Most of the route is a footpath, although a short section has been destroyed by gravel workings.

The golden expanse of Camber Sands which was once served by its own railway. ROBIN JONES

Ford railmotor set on the Pagham Harbour embankment, c.1924. The innovative use of railmotors on Colonel Stephens' light railways became a characteristic feature of several. CSRM

Holman Fred Stephens as Lieutenant Colonel. CSRM

SELSEY TRAMWAY AND STEPHENS THE COMMANDING OFFICER

After the Rye & Camber Tramway, the next venture for Holman Stephens was the West Sussex Railway, which began life in 1897 under the banner of the Hundred of Manhood and Selsey Tramway, so as to circumvent the regulations governing convention lines of the day.

The seaside town of Selsey lies at the southernmost point of the Manhood peninsula, and is almost cut off from mainland Sussex by the sea. Indeed, at one time Selsey was inaccessible at flood tide, and a boat was stationed at the ferry to take horses and passengers to and from Sidlesham.

Today's B2145 is the only road in and out of the town crossing a bridge over the water inlet at Pagham Harbour at a point known as 'the ferry'.

The Hundred of Manhood and Selsey Tramway was formed to construct a

standard gauge railway from Chichester to Selsey, and was incorporated as a limited company on April 29, 1896.

The imminent 1896 Light Railways Act led Chichester politicians and businessmen to discuss whether it might be worth building a light railway to Selsey eight miles to the south.

Looking into the proposed legislation, which received royal assent on August 14, 1896, the promoters, led by Lewes estate agent H J Powell, supported by the local Clayton family, worked out that it would be possible to get

authorisation much more simply under the Railway Construction Facilities Act 1864. By structuring the line as a tramway, the numerous public road level crossings would not require the special safety arrangements required for railway operation, hence the company title which included the word tramway.

Indeed, it was unusual for a railway – or a tramway for that matter – to be incorporated without statutory backing. It could be allowed only if the land over which it ran was privately acquired, although this forced a slightly indirect route, and the roads crossed with the consent of the local highways authority.

Holman Stephens was appointed as its engineer and subsequently as its manager. Indeed, he had started work on it in 1895, before the company was registered. He used lightweight flat-bottomed rail for its construction over what was mainly a flat landscape, with fairly basic rolling stock.

As with the Rye & Camber Tramway, he brought in Mancktelow Brothers of Hormonden, which had built the stations on the Hawkshurst line, to erect similar structures on his latest venture.

The tramway started from a point a little to the south of the London, Brighton & South Coast Railway station at Chichester and ran south for the 7¼ miles to Selsey. The only major engineering feature was a lifting bridge over the Chichester Canal.

During the line's history, seven steam locomotives hauled passenger trains over it. The first, *Chichester*, an 0-4-2ST, arrived with the name *Wembley* having worked there previously, and the engine continued to be known by that name for some time. It had been built in 1865 by Dodds of Rotherham as an 0-6-0ST.

The only new steam locomotive supplied to the line was *Selsey*, a 2-4-2T built in 1897 by Peckett & Sons. The first trains ran on August 27, 1897, and the following year, the tramway was extended by half a mile from Selsey Town to the beach. However, this extension was taken out of use by 1908.

The cost of both land purchases and construction were said to be on the low side, and Stephens' subsequent career involved several local lines often run on minimal finance. During Edwardian times, the line prospered.

Following a fierce storm on December 15, 1910, the line along with 2000 acres of land was flooded by the sea after an embankment failed at Pagham Harbour, leaving the track 12ft under water in places. The embankment was not reinstated so work had to be carried out to raise the line up to 10ft above the waters, while a horse bus filled the gap in services between Mill Pond Half and Ferry station.

In 1913, the directors proposed an extension from Hunston to West Itchenor and East Wittering, using a Light Railway Order which would regularise the legal status of the tramway, although the track would need to be rebuilt and the level crossing improved. However, due to the outbreak of the First World War, the order was not granted by the Light Railway commissioners until 1915, and the improvements could not be made during the conflict.

'MODERN TRACTION'

After the First World War, with motor transport in the ascendancy, and rural light railways suffering from declining passenger numbers and freight levels everywhere, the line was hit hard by competition from buses. Southdown Motor Services had been formed in 1915 and was running timetabled bus services locally, and increasingly passengers preferred to take the bus—at a higher fare. Rail passenger numbers fell from 102,292 in 1919 to 31,352 in 1924.

Prompted by Stephens, new owners, predominantly his friend Mr H Montague Bates, bought the tramway company in 1919-20. Stephens became all but the sole owner when the shares were bequeathed or sold to him. Although reasonable wealthy through inheritances, in most of the railway companies with which he would become involved Stephens normally bought only sufficient shares to allow him to qualify as a director if needed.

Stephens looked at ways of reducing operating expenses, and in 1921 trialled a Wolseley-Siddeley petrol railcar on the line. It did not enter service, but in 1924 the tramway acquired two railcars built on Ford Model T chassis, with bodies by Edmunds of Thetford.

These operated together, back-to-back with a truck for luggage and parcels between them. They had rails on the roof to contain additional parcels stowed there.

Two further railcars were acquired from the Shefflex Motor Company of Tinsley in 1928 and they also operated as a unit with a truck between. The railcars

The 'enemy' awaits: 1866-built Manning Wardle No.7 0-6-0ST *Morous* with a rake of wagons crosses the road at Ferry station as a car stops to let it pass. It would be motor transport, particularly buses, that would kill off the Selsey Tramway along with most of the other light railways and later many country rail routes that were part of the national network. CSRM

Selsey engine shed with 2-4-2T No.2 *Selsey*, 0-6-0ST No.5 *Ringing Rock*, 0-6-0ST No.3 *Sidlesham* and 0-4-2T No.1 *Chichester* on July 16, 1927. CSRM

were provided with a crude timber buffer beam in front of the radiator, as protection.

STEPHENS THE COLONEL

At this point, it may be timely to relate how Holman Stephens acquired the army rank for which made

him a household name in railway circles and for which he is best known today.

His teenage interest in the armed forces never abated and by May 1896 he had been given a commission as a second lieutenant in the Volunteer Forces.

Furthermore, the commission was with what else but an engineering unit, is the shape of the 1st Sussex Royal Engineers (Volunteers). He showed the same degree of enthusiasm for the military as he had for light railways and earned several promotions, both temporary and permanent.

Former Shropshire & Montgomeryshire Light Railway Manning Wardle 0-6-0ST No.7 *Morous* at Selsey with a mixed train. CSRM

Manning Wardle 0-6-0ST, No.5 *Ringing Rock* which was built in 1883 and bought secondhand from industrial service, stands with a passenger train alongside the Ford railmotor set around 1924. The initial coaching stock fleet consisted of three bogie saloon coaches from Falcons, acquired in 1897. A similar coach was purchased from Hurst Nelson about 1900. In 1910 three four-wheel coaches were acquired from the Lambourn Valley Railway and four four-wheelers were bought from the London, Chatham and Dover Railway (LCDR). Finally, in 1931 two six-wheel coaches were acquired from the Southern Railway, probably for summer Saturdays when the railcars would be inadequate; they had been built for the LCDR. CSRM

comotive 2-4-2T No.2 *Selsey* in the platform at
ichester with crew and station staff, c.1905. CSRM

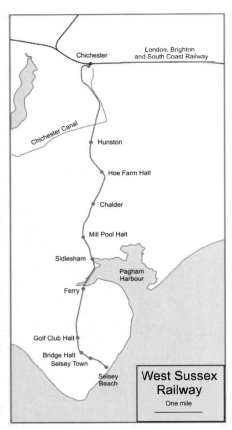

Map of the West Sussex Railway, originally known as the Hundred of Manhood and Selsey Tramway.

He was made first lieutenant in 1897, captain in 1898. Then, in 1905, he became captain with the 2nd Cinque Ports, Royal Garrison Artillery (Volunteers). The volunteer forces were reshuffled in 1908, when Stephens was made a major as commanding officer of the Kent (Fortress) Royal Engineers.

After the First World War began, Stephens was temporarily promoted to lieutenant colonel in April 1915 as the size of the companies under his command increased. Originally having responsibility for the defence of the Thames and Medway estuaries, these companies were next upgraded for service overseas.

However, in 1916, sheer pressure of work left Stephens facing a choice between his military and railway careers. Accordingly, he stepped down from his Army post and transferred to the Territorial Reserve forces on April 1 that year. Soon afterwards he became a major again, this time to command a volunteer unit: the Weald of Kent Battalion of the Kent Volunteer Fencibles.

In 1923, he took command of the Sussex (Fortress) RE Territorials, only

for it to be disbanded two years later. No matter; the men along with Stephens still in charge were switched to the Cinque Ports (Fortress) RE.

While in 1921 Stephens had been gazetted as Lieutenant Colonel, out of traditional courtesy he was always addressed at Colonel Stephens. He considered his military volunteer role both his patriotic duty and a hobby, but as a secondary activity to his day job.

FATAL DERAILMENT

Disaster struck on September 3, 1923, when the 8.15am three-coach train to Chichester came off the track near Golf Club Halt, with the driver being killed outright and the fireman injured.

The subsequent inquest returned a verdict of accidental death. However, the jury indirectly loaded the blame onto Stephens as the line's engineer because the track was inadequate.

With the 1915 Light Railway Order time expired, in order to give the line legal status, the Ministry of Transport issued a new order – the West Sussex Railway Certificate 1924. It authorised a new company, the West Sussex Railway

A satirical postcard of the Hundred of Manhood and Selsey Tramway from around 1907. The line was known locally as the Selsey Tram and sometimes called The Siddlesham Snail. Sidlesham station's nameboard originally perpetuated the old spelling 'Siddlesham'. A song was written criticising the line. The verse ran: "The Siddlesham snail, the Siddlesham snail, the boilers burst, she's off the rail, the Siddlesham snail!"

OUR LOCAL EXPRESS.
Chichester to Selsey

Company, to take over and rebuild the line. It eventually completed the takeover in 1928, taking on the line's debts and liabilities in the process. Both the old and new company were dominated by Stephens and his colleagues.

This line had been surveyed by the builders of the Romney, Hythe & Dymchurch Railway in the early 1920s when they were looking for somewhere to build their miniature line, which ended

up in Kent. Despite being otherwise ideal for their purposes, Stephens' line was discounted because of the number of road crossings which would have been prohibitively expensive to either gate or bridge.

CLOSURE AFTER 39 YEARS
Montague Bates died in 1928 and Colonel Stephens himself followed three years later. Stephens' so-called 'outdoor

Because the locomotive used by the contractor that built the line could not access the southern section because the bridge over the Chichester Canal had not been completed, it was hauled by a traction engine to its place of work. The locomotive, later named *Chichester*, ran on rails placed on their sides in the roadway; workmen progressively moved the rails to the front of it as it made its slow movement behind the traction engine.

The lifting bridge over the Chichester Canal as seen in 1897.

assistant' William Austen took over and kept his light railway empire going wherever possible.

He invited the Southern Railway to take over the line and improve it. A survey was made with this end in mind, but the big railway decided against it. Having lost heart because of the increasing competition from buses, the directors closed the line from January 14, 1935, bringing 39 years of local transport history to a close.

Very little remains of the railway today. Apart from the half-mile section alongside Pagham Harbour, where the track was raised following the flooding in 1911, a quarter-mile section is now a farm track between the harbour and Selsey Golf Club, and a further quarter-mile section is now a public footpath west of Hunston village. The northern part of this path ends at the abutments of the now-defunct tramway bridge across the Chichester Canal. The platforms of Hunston and Chalder stations can also still be detected – although both are now badly overgrown.

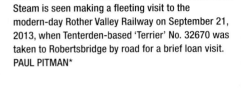

Chapter 4

Steam is seen making a fleeting visit to the modern-day Rother Valley Railway on September 21, 2013, when Tenterden-based 'Terrier' No. 32670 was taken to Robertsbridge by road for a brief loan visit. PAUL PITMAN*

Heading across a level crossing east of Bodiam en route to Tenterden Town on September 9, 2014, is Hunslet Austerity 0-6-0ST No. 3791 of 1952 *Holman F Stephens*. One of a batch of 14 built in 1952-53 as war reserve stock, and originally numbered WD191, it entered service on the Bicester Military Railway where it carried the name *Black Knight*. Placed into store in 1962, it was withdrawn from service in August 1968. Sold out of Army service, it arrived on the KESR in February 1972 and was later renamed there in honour of the line's engineer, general manager and managing director. ROBIN JONES

KENT & EAST SUSSEX LIGHT RAILWAY: THE STEPHENS EPITOME?

Winding its way through hop-picking country, the Kent & East Sussex Railway is widely considered to be the most perfect example of a 'typical' Colonel Stephens line, both in his day and also in the heritage era.

The Kent & East Sussex Railway is a classic example of lines that were built 'on the cheap' under the provisions of the 1896 Light Railways Act to link sparsely-populated rural backwaters to the national network. It eventually became part of the light railway empire of the legendary Colonel Stephens, to who a museum at the line's Tenterden Town station is dedicated.

The town of Tenterden, which today has a population of nearly 8000, lies on the edge of the Weald, overlooking

The entrance to Tenterden Town station, the headquarters of today's Kent & East Sussex Railway.

The line's 1959-built Class 108 DMU waits at Tenterden Town station. ROBIN JONES

Construction of the Rother Valley Railway near Tenterden around 1900. CSRM

the valley of the River Rother. Its name is derived from the Old English Tenetwaradenn, meaning a denn or swine-pasture for the men of Thanet.

It began to thrive on the local wood industry from around the 14th century, and had the advantage over its Wealden neighbours in having access to the sea. Much of what is now Romney Marsh was under water, and ships docked at nearby Smallhythe.

Timber from the forests was used to build ships, and in 1449 Tenterden was incorporated into the Confederation of Cinque Ports as an arm of Rye. However, its river today is no longer navigable to large vessels and its status as a wool manufacturing centre has long since been lost.

By the middle of the 19th century, very rural Tenterden found itself in the centre of a triangle of railway lines. The South Eastern Railway opened its line from Redhill to Tonbridge on July 12, 1841, extending to Headcorn on August 31, 1842 and to Ashford on December 1. 1843.

The company's line from Ashford to Hastings opened on February 13, 1851. The line between Tonbridge and Hastings was opened as far as Tunbridge Wells on November 24, 1846, Robertsbridge on September 1, 1851, and to St Leonards on February 1, 1852, having negotiated running rights over the London, Brighton & South Coast Railway's line to Hastings.

The original scheme to link Ashford and Hastings involved a route via Headcorn and Tenterden, but the government of the day insisted on the more southerly route. A proposed railway from Headcorn via Cranbrook to Tenterden failed to obtain statutory powers in 1855, as had an 1846 proposal for the Weald of Kent Railway from Paddock Wood via Cranbrook and Tenterden to Hythe, and likewise an 1882 plan for a roadside tramway from Headcorn to Tenterden.

The Cranbrook & Paddock Wood Railway obtained powers to construct the northern section of the Weald of Kent Railway in 1877. This would allow the transportation of agricultural produce and livestock from low-lying land adjacent to Wittersham Road to a better main line connection. An extension to Goudhurst opened in 1892 and to Hawkhurst in 1893.

Proposals for a Tenterden Railway were drawn up in 1892, running from Maidstone to Hastings via Headcorn, Tenterden, and Appledore. The section from Headcorn to Appledore was authorised in the same year and agreement was reached in 1896 with the South Eastern Railway over the operation of the line.

However, six years later, the plans were scrapped in favour of extending the Cranbrook & Paddock Wood Railway to Tenterden and Appledore. Townsfolk of the former were again to be left without a railway though, as the scheme floundered because it was deemed too expensive, even though it was also backed by the South Eastern Railway.

What was needed was a rural line to be built 'on the cheap'...

Pressure from businessmen and landowners in Bodiam and Northiam led to a scheme for yet another line to be drawn up under the banner of the Rother Valley Railway, after the river whose course it would follow. The Rother Valley Railway duly received authorisation under its own Act of Parliament in 1896, a few months before the Light Railways Act was passed.

The directors then successfully applied to have the railway brought under the auspices of the new light railway legislation and it was duly built under the latter Act.

Stephens was appointed as the line's engineer and had marked out the route by November 1897. The contract for the construction of the standard gauge line was won by London and Scottish Contract Corporation, who sub-contracted the work to Godfrey and Siddelow. Building began in 1898.

However, progress was slowed by the lack of investment and by one contractor going bankrupt.

Stephens became the line's general manager in 1899 and its managing director the following year.

TENTERDEN CONNECTED AT LAST

On January 9, 1900, it was reported that the track from Robertsbridge Junction to Tenterden was completed. A wind pump was provided at Robertsbridge to supply water for locomotives. More delays were caused by flooding in the valley that February, but its first section opened to freight on March 26 and to passengers on April 2. The original Tenterden station, later renamed Rolvenden, lay two miles from the town, so the frustration

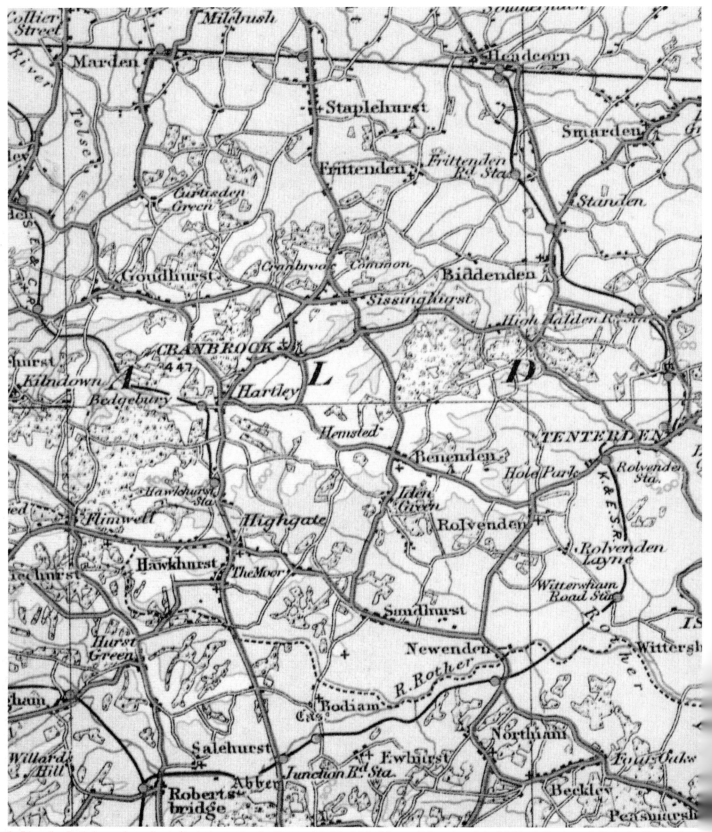

An Edwardian Bartholomew four-miles-to-the-inch map showing the completed Kent & East Sussex Railway from Robertsbridge to Headcorn via Tenterden Town and linking lines.

of many residents remained unabated. Also, townsfolk were concerned that the opening of the light railway from Robertsbridge in the west would prevent a more heavily engineered line being built from Headcorn in the north. Around 60 passengers travelled on that first train, a somewhat lukewarm reception.

The building of the Cranbrook & Tenterden Light Railway from Cranbrook via Benenden to the Tenterden terminus of the Rother Valley Railway, and to extend one-and-a-half miles into the town of Tenterden itself, had been authorised in December of the previous year. However, only the extension into

Tenterden Town was built, opening on April 15, 1903.

The first train from the newly-rename Rolvenden to Tenterden carried 312 schoolchildren, along with Sir Myles Fenton, Stephens, and other dignitaries. The South Eastern & Chatham Railway (SECR) wanted rid of any obligation to build the Tenterden Railway, and reached an agreement with the Rother Valley Railway for the latter to build and run the line from Tenterden to Headcorn. The SECR agreed to make up any operating losses in exchange for an option to purchase the line at any time within the next 21 years from the date of opening.

The Rother Valley Railway changed its name to the Kent & East Sussex Light Railway in 1904.

Its northern extension opened to traffic on May 15, 1905. However, the Rother Valley would push forward no more: authorised schemes to reach to Rye, Cranbook, Pevensey and Maidstone came to nothing.

The majority of the locomotives bought for the line were, as at other Stephens railways, second-hand.

Hawthorn Leslie 2-4-0Ts No. 2420 of 1899 and No. 2421 of 1899 were both bought new for the opening of the line, and became the line's No. 1 *Tenterden* and No. 2 *Northiam* respectively. In 1917, *No.2* was loaned to the Weston, Clevedon & Portishead Railway for a year, and in 1923 it was borrowed for seven years by the East Kent Light Railway. The locomotive also enjoyed big screen stardom in the film *Oh, Mr Porter!* which was shot on the Basingstoke & Alton Light Railway. Both locomotives were scrapped in 1941.

No. 3 Bodiam was of a type that was to become a trademark of the KESR both then and now.

An LBSCR 'Terrier' built in 1872 as No. 70 *Poplar*, it was bought for the light railway in 1901. Withdrawn in 1931, it was back in action two years later using parts cannibalised from sister No. 5 *Rolvenden*.

LBSCR 'Terrier' 0-6-0T No. 70 *Poplar* which became the light railway's No. 3 *Bodiam* and is now part of the Kent & East Sussex Railway fleet today. CSRM

Jumping ahead in our narrative, the locomotive appeared in the film The Loves of Joanna Godden which filmed at Lydd in 1947. Working on the Hayling Island branch in its latter British Railways day, it was withdrawn in November 1963 as No. 32670 and bought privately for the heritage era KESR, where it remains today.

After its opening and completion throughout to Headcorn, the KESR settled down into a largely-profitable concern, and in 1910, second-hand but more comfortable steam-heated carriages were obtained, and were superior in their time to many coaches in use on mainly lines. More locomotives were also obtained.

In 1913, a parliamentary study on the need to improve standards of rural transport praised the railway.

The KESR came under government control when the First World War broke out in 1914,, as did most railways. It was released from government control in 1921 and £1487 in compensation was paid – totally inadequate to make up for the wear and tear combined with low maintenance that the line had suffered during the war.

Also, the end of the war released a huge fleet of army lorries and buses on

Hawthorn Leslie 2-4-0T No.1 *Tenterden* was bought new in 1899 for the opening of the Rother Valley Railway. It was withdrawn for overhaul in 1938 and scrapped in 1941. CSRM

'Terrier' No. 3 *Bodiam* heads a train into Tenterden Town station on its opening day in 1903. CSRM

to the second-hand market, making road transport in rural communities for both passengers and freight a cheaper option.

Not to be easily outdone, the enterprising Stephens introduced petrol-engined railmotors to the KESR to supplement the steam services. In this respect he was very much a pioneer in a railway world in which internal combustion was starting to be seen as the future, as opposed to steam which was costlier to run.

Stephens maintained the view that light railways introduced to serve the needs of rural communities must be built and run at low cost. When building the Rye and Camber Tramway, he told the authorities that he wished to use 'an oil motor on a bogie passenger car' to operate the service.

However, this was a step many years ahead of his time, as the internal combustion engine was less than a decade old,

and so a small steam locomotive had to suffice.

During the First World War, lorry and bus technology leapt forward and Stephens, who had not given up experimenting with it, tried out an Edwardian Wolseley-Siddeley car chassis that had been adapted as a rail lorry and then as a bus on the KESR.

Again, the forward-thinking colonel was ahead of his day in terms of world transport technology, because by then only a few railways in North America and one French manufacturer were carrying out similar experimentation.

He then bought some cheap mass produced one-ton Ford Model T lorry chassis mounted with bus bodies and used them in back-to-back pairs to avoid the reversing problem.

The first Ford railmotor was allocated to the KESR and may have entered service on February 15, 1923. These

vehicles attracted widespread attention as novelties: a Pathe News film made for screening in early cinemas shows the railmotor as it first entered service on the line.

A second railmotor set was delivered in April 1924, built by Edmonds of Thetford.

Costs savings produced by the railmotors became increasingly attractive and they eventually took over around a third of all mileage. During the General Strike of 1926 and its coal strike the railmotors accounted for more than half the KESR services.

In December 1927, Stephens ordered a new railmotor set, this time from Shefflex Motors Ltd of Tinsley, Sheffield. However, road transport was still very much winning the day by the Twenties: passenger numbers in 1913 were around 105,000 but by 1922 the figure had dropped to 68,000. Dividends to shareholders fell and investment in the line was repeatedly postponed.

Having lost much of its general merchandise freight, the KESR survived mainly through coal and mineral traffic, and by Stephens cutting costs. The busiest time was the annual hop-picking season when crowds arrived from London by train.

Stephens exerted pressure on the government not to include light railway in the Grouping of 1923, and so they continued their independent existence albeit in the face of increasing odds.

By 1924, the section from Tenterden to Headcorn was operating at a loss, even though the western section still made

London & South Western Railway Beyer Peacock 'Ilfracombe Goods' 0-6-0T No. 1208 of 1873 which was bought second-hand in 1910 to become No. 7 *Rother* and scrapped in 1939, derailed outside Tenterden in 1910. CSRM

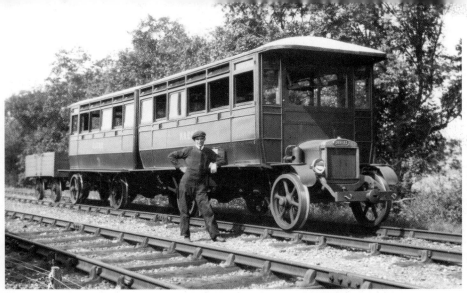

The Shellfex railmotor set of 1927 is seen with driver Nelson Wood, possibly Rolvenden, in 1934. CSRM

small profits. The Southern Railway was liable to cover the operating losses, as the successor to the SECR under the terms of the Act of Parliament for the construction of the northern section of the line, but even with this financial input they could not be sustained.

The first railmotor set was withdrawn in 1932, No.2 five years later and the Shefflex set in 1938.

SUCCESSOR TO THE COLONEL

Stephens suffered a stroke at the end of January 1930, affecting his movement and speech. He suffered a second several months later, and was admitted to a nursing home in London, but discharged himself and sought convalescence in Hastings. However, because he had difficulty in talking, he was taken in at the Lord Warden Hotel in Dover, where he was known by staff.

A workaholic almost to the end, Stephens continued to visit his railway empire, assisted by his staff, until to April 1931, but on October 23, 1931, eight days

short of his 63rd birthday, he was found dead in bed at the Lord Warden after suffering a heart attack.

Stephens' funeral took place in St Peter's Church, Hammersmith, just round the corner from the firmer family home in Hammersmith Terrace, and he was buried in the family grave at Brompton cemetery. The funeral was attended by senior railway figures including Richard Maunsell, the chief mechanical engineer of both the SECR and then the Southern Railway, and Major-General Gilbert Savil Szlumper, the penultimate general manager of the Southern Railway.

The management of Stephens' railway empire was taken over by his long-time 'outdoor assistant' William Henry Austen. Said to have been a hardworking and versatile manager, Austen lacked the charisma and innovation of his predecessor and never commanded the same level of affection from his staff.

Communications between the pair were said over 40 years to have been

somewhat like a master-and-servant relationship. Planning a visit to his parents at their riverside home in Hammersmith in August 1895, Stephens wrote "Can you let my man have the servant's room?" and on Boat Race day in March 1897, he said "May I bring my man with me? He has never seen the race and would appreciate it I think".

However, Stephens was godfather to Austen's only son, who also bore his name. Stephens never socialised with Austen in the way that he did with Szlumper and other influential members of his London clubs though, probably because of Austen's humble origins. As an aside, Austen was a cousin of the Soviet spy Guy Burgess.

Losses on the KESE soared to the point where it entered receivership in 1932 and Austen was appointed official receiver. He looked more and more to the Southern Railway for help, and received it in the form of deferred debts. Locomotives and engineering services were hired but during the Thirties the one-time shining example of a rural railway had increasingly slumped into decrepitude.

The whole line was re-laid with 60 pounds per yard in 1939.

SECOND WORLD WAR AND AFTER

When the war began on September 1, 1939, the K&ESR again came under government control, and was placed under the Railway Operating Division of the Royal Engineers. With rail-mounted battery guns brought in by a War Department, former GWR Dean Goods 0-6-0 were stationed at Rolvenden and Wittersham.

This rural backwater line became an alternative supply route to the south coast, and relieved some of the pressure on Ashford. Components for Operation PLUTO (see Chapter 2) were carried.

The national drive for scrap led to most of the KESR's surplus rolling stock being scrapped, but on the other hand, around 10 miles of the track were relaid. In the build up to D-Day, heavy troop trains were worked over the line, along with special trains carrying materials to build aerodromes which were run between Headcorn and Tenterden. Southern Railway locomotives were drafted in to help with the increased volume of traffic, especially through trains, the movements of which were often shrouded in essential secrecy.

While the KESR had escaped the Grouping of 1923, it was not so fortunate with the nationalisation of Britain railways from January 1, 1948. The Transport Act 1947 ended its independence which had started with Stephens.

At nationalisation, one of the surviving two locomotives and all but the newest rolling stock were scrapped. The line

Modern traction sandwiched between old campaigners: Rolvenden station in 1932, with 2-4-0T No. 1 *Tenterden*, Ford railmotor No. 2, and 2-4-0T No. 2 *Northiam*. CSRM

No. 7 *Rother* stands at the head of a train in Tenterden Town station with Ford railmotor set No. 1 in the loop. CSRM

Ford railmotor set No. 2 at Headcorn Junction. CSRM

Hoppers wait at Junction Road Halt in the line's heyday. Also known as Junction Road (for Hawkhurst), it was located on the eastern side of the level crossing across the B2244 Junction Road near the hamlet of Udiam. The line through Junction Road Halt may be revived if plans by the modern-day Rother Valley Railway are given the green light to rebuild the line from Robertsbridge to Bodiam. CSRM

continued to be run as two sections, either side of Tenterden Town, and the track was again re-laid to a higher standard using rails salvaged from the Elham Valley Railway. Efforts were made to encourage tourism with day excursion bookings from London, and staffing of stations was increased. Sadly, these initiatives did not produce an increase in passengers – with traffic increasingly ebbing away to the roads. During a typical week in 1953, only 118 passengers travelled on 90 trains, many of which ran empty.

British Railways had contemplated closure as early as 1948 and the final regular passenger train, the 5.50pm from Robertsbridge to Headcorn, ran on January 2, 1954. The train was comprised of six corridor coaches specially brought from Ashford for the occasion. LBSCR 'Terrier' 0-6-0T No. 32655 headed the train with sister No. 32678 at the rear. No. 32655 was then replaced by SECR O1 0-6-0T No. 31065 and No. 2678 banked the train to St Michael's. The 'Terriers' then ran back to Robertsbridge with a carriage between them to reduce the weight on the bridges, as double heading on that section was banned.

It was decided to keep freight running on the Robertsbridge to Tenterden Town section while the section north to Headcorn was lifted throughout 1955. The Rother Valley section was subjected to rationalisation, with the buildings at Rolveden taken down.

Two freight trains a day were run, with hop-pickers' specials running until 1958, along with occasional passenger traffic in the form of railtours. After October 17, 1955, only the morning freight continued.

Despite the fact that the railway now appeared to be living on borrowed time, dieselisation made its presence felt when, in 1957, Drewry shunter No. 11220 was successfully tried, and this along with 11223, not the line's trademark 'Terriers', were the regular locomotives for the final years of operation. In 1958, Hastings Diesel Electric Multiple Unit No. 1002 underwent load tests between Bodiam and Northiam.

The final passenger train over the line before closure between Robertsbridge and Tenterden Town was a Locomotive

A third-class hop picker's ticket from London Bridge to Bodian via Robertsbridge in 1938. CSRM

Club of Great Britain railtour on June 11, 1961, the day after the last freight, the 7.55am from Robertsbridge, had run. Next day, the line closed, the short section between the main line and Hodsons Mill at Robertsbridge, which survived as a private siding until January 1, 1970.

REVIVED BY VOLUNTEERS

During the period of the KESR's independence and insolvency in the 1920s and 1930s, railway enthusiasts and others had become attracted to the line's eccentricities and uniqueness. In 1948 the magazine *Punch* was sufficiently moved by the loss of independence to commission a poem illustrated by the eminent cartoonist Roland Emmett called The Farmers' Train. Such sentiment showed how the line had become a local, indeed a national, institution and soon after closure the Kent & East Sussex Railway Preservation Society was formed with the object of preserving the line.

The revivalists fought a 13-year battle before the first trains were run. Protracted legal tussles with the then Minister of Transport Barbara Castle halted demolition, but the line was only saved when the society had to drop the Bodiam-Robertsbridge section – with its three road crossings – from its revival plans. This section, which included the line's surviving main line connection, was lifted and became abandoned.

Negotiations then proceeded quickly and the present registered charity took over the railway in 1973. Years of neglect and the original lightly-engineered nature of the line meant that the task had to be tackled in stages.

The first two miles at Tenterden were opened on February 3, 1974. A major renewal of a river bridge enabled an extension by 1977 to Wittersham Road. Further consolidation was then necessary but Northiam was finally reached in 1990 and Bodiam on April 2, 2000, exactly a century to the day after the line first opened under Stephens, and making a total of 10½ miles.

ROTHER VALLEY RAILWAY AND THE MISSING LINK

Under its memorandum and articles of association, the Kent & East Sussex Railway Company has powers to operate the railway between Tenterden and Robertsbridge. However, it has no plans to extend west of Bodiam.

A separate company, the Rother Valley Railway (East Sussex) Ltd, was formed on May 22, 1991 to rebuild the 3½ miles of missing line between Bodiam and Robertsbridge and has since simplified its name to Rother Valley Railway Ltd.

Once linked up to the KESR, a 14-mile heritage railway be created, and it would also have a main line connection. Since 1991, the railway has been acquiring parts of the trackbed as and when

LBSCR A1X 'Terrier' 0-6-0ST No. 32678 with a Kent & East Sussex Railway mixed train at Robertsbridge in the early 1950s. Built at Brighton in July 1880, it worked the line's last regular passenger train in January 1954, and was withdrawn from Brighton (75A) in October 1963 with more than 1.4 million miles on the clock. Saved for preservation, it arrived at the revived Kent & East Sussex Railway in 1988 and is now a much-loved member of the railway's steam locomotive fleet. CSRM

Crowds throng Tenterden Town station for the last train in 1961. CSRM

The end is nigh: A busy Robertsbridge station on January 2, 1954, the last day of BR's passenger service on the KESR. On the main line is Schools class 4-4-0 No. 30905 *Tonbridge* on a Hastings to Charing Cross express, and in the bay platform, A1X 'Terrier' 0-6-0T No. 32655 has arrived with a train from Tenterden Town and Headcorn, just hours before the service ceased. If plans by the modern-day Rother Valley Railway bear fruit, Robertsbridge will once again be the terminus for trains from Tenterden. BEN BROOKSBANK*

The light railway's original No. 3 *Bodiam*, LBSCR A1X 0-6-0T 'Terrier' No. 32670 stands at Tenterden Town in June 2011. It was withdrawn when its 10-year boiler certificate expired in January 2017 and was despatched to the Weybourne workshops of North Norfolk Railway Engineering for overhaul. It is planned to return it to service in 2022 as No. 3 for the planned Terrier 150 programme marking its 150th birthday – in 1872 it became the first of William Stroudley's legendary class of 0-6-0Ts to be built – and for which a £150,000 appeal has been launched at www.terriertrust.org.uk. It and sister No. 2678 are the oldest in the Kent & East Sussex Railway's fleet and representatives of a type that has been synonymous with the line for more than a century. Terrier 150 will also highlight the impact of the 'Terriers' on the KESR, other lines once run by Colonel Stephens and railways more generally. PETER SKUCE*

possible, and liaising with the various authorities to ensure that the necessary planning consents and orders will be granted.

A base has been established in the yard at Robertsbridge station alongside the London Charing Cross-Hastings main line to which it is connected. It is being transformed into a steam railway complex with station, five-coach platform, engine and carriage sheds, and other facilities.

So far, half a mile of track has been laid between Robertsbridge and Northtridge Street.

There are three road crossings to be reinstated including the A21 Robertsbridge bypass – the original stumbling block and major reason why the revivalists back in the 1960s could not acquire the section.

Negotiations between the modern-day RVR, whose benefactors are providing

the finance for the scheme, and two farming families have been ongoing for years. The two-mile gap, between the western end of the KESR at Austen's Bridge and Northbridge Street, is across fields that the families own. The big obstacle now is the impasse between the RVR and the families who, at the time of writing in summer 2020, were still refusing sell the part of their land over which the missing link would be built.

Details of an independent report showed that if the gap was bridged and a 14-mile line between Robertsbridge and Tenterden created, the annual benefit to the local economy would be more than £4 million. Up to 75 jobs would be created and train operator Southeastern, which serves Robertsbridge, would accrue additional yearly revenues of £600,000.

Conservative MP Huw Merriman, whose Bexhill & Battle constituency includes the entire RVR and part of the KESR, said that he believed the project had the potential to increase tourism.

Following eight years at the planning stage, an application for a Transport & Works Act order that would enable the link to be built has been submitted by the RVR to the government. A total of 13 reports and schedules required for the order application covering nearly 1000 pages, were finalised and submitted.

Highways England and Rother District Council both approved the plans for the A21 level crossing, but the Office of Rail and Road has sought further information. It has reviewed the proposals to consider whether they justify a departure from its policy of no new (or reinstated) level crossings.

A Department for Transport public inquiry into the Rother Valley Railway (Bodiam to Robertsbridge Junction) Order under the Transport and Works Act 1992 was subsequently arranged for May 26, 2020, and was expected to last for 16 days. However, it was postponed because of the Covid-19 pandemic that plunged Britain and the world into crisis. At the time of writing no new date had been set.

A splendid archetypal Colonel Stephens empire light railway summer scene: LSBSCR A1X 'Terrier' 0-6-0T No. 32678 hauls a rake of vintage wooden-bodies carriages along the Kent & East Sussex Railway. Originally outshopped from Brighton works in 1880 as No.78 *Knowle*, this locomotive was the last 'Terrier' in BR service, hauling the final train over the lightly-laid West Quay lines at Newhaven and the severely weight-restricted swing bridge over the River Ouse on August 10, 1963. First preserved on static display at the Butlins holiday camp in Minehead from where it was purchased by the KESR in 1975, it is now owned by the Terrier Trust. KESR

I have no doubt that the restoration of the missing link, completing Stephen's original Rother Valley Railway, would be a massive boon to local tourism, economies and heritage, and would be the ultimate showcase for, and monument to, the work of this legendary 'people's railway' pioneer who found himself at the threshold between the Victorian steam age and the dawn of the road motor transport era. Tenterden would once again have a railway that would link it to the capital, and who knows – maybe those hop-pickers specials from the capital might return!

ALONG THE 21ST CENTURY KENT & EAST SUSSEX RAILWAY

Tenterden Town station is the headquarters of the heritage line and contains some of its principal buildings including the carriage and wagon workshop. Facilities for visitors include a shop, refreshment rooms and a small children's playground.

The station is also the perfect location for the excellent award-winning Colonel Stephens Museum, as described in Chapter 17.

As the train leaves Tenterden, the line falls steeply away towards the marshes at an average gradient of 1-in-50 for over a mile (the train has to work very hard

British Thomson-Houston diesel electric locomotive No. 40 is the surviving member of a class of three built in 1931 for the internal system at the Ford plant in Dagenham, where it was numbered 1. Withdrawn on July 5, 1966, it arrived at Tenterden two days later. It was hired to James Hodson & Sons, Robertsbridge Flour Mills in 1967 and it hauled the last train from Robertsbridge to Bodiam in February 1972 prior to the track being lifted on that section. It may not be a petrol railmotor, but Colonel Stephens the great innovator would almost certainly have approved. KESR

on its return). The Wealden scenery across the valley is particularly fine as the line crosses the Cranbrook road about halfway down. The descent continues and the line curves sharply to the left at Orpin's Farm where the track levels out and crosses the main road before running into Rolvenden station, 1½ miles from Tenterden Town.

Rolvenden was always the headquarters of the locomotive works, which remain on the site. However, the original buildings have long since gone, the site covered by the present wood yard. The village of Rolvenden is 1½ miles away, and containing some attractive cottages and a church that is pleasantly situated. Lovers of historic vehicles will find the CM Booth collection in the centre of the village of great interest and a short distance outside the town is the oldest post mill in Kent.

The next station, Wittersham Road, is reached through marshlands collectively known as the Rother Levels. To the right a series of channels dug at right angles to the railway were used to farm crayfish and on the left, in the woodland, if you are lucky you may see wild boar which are also farmed. The terrain generally is very wet and until comparatively recently was subject to frequent flooding. The most characteristic trees along the lineside are willows.

The trains cross over the New Mill Channel, a tributary of the Rother, which now runs alongside for several hundred yards and is home to many swans here, particularly in the winter months.

The line curves gently into Wittersham Road, a station apparently in the middle of nowhere, which actually handled quite heavy agricultural traffic. However, Wittersham itself is nearly three miles away and Rolvenden Layne is actually the nearest village, being a long mile the other way. The station had an exciting time during the Second World War when it was the depot site for the aforementioned large rail mounted gun that fired at occupied France. The ammunition store for this is still to be seen on the corner of the picnic site.

The sidings here are used by the permanent way department and house a growing collection of track maintenance machines.

Starting from Wittersham Road, the train is faced with a steep but short climb as the line follows the contours of the land rather than cutting through it.

Over the summit the line now falls towards the Hexden Channel and the Rother whose valley is very wide and open at this point. The landscape is dotted by Romney sheep and you will often see turf-cutting as you cross this area. To the left the channel and the Rother join and sweep out past the Isle of Oxney on which Wittersham stands towards Romney Marsh and the sea at Rye.

The December Santa season on the Kent & East Sussex brings with it the opportunity to photograph in stunning winter light. The late running 2.58pm from Northiam, hauled by USA 0-6-0T No. 65, catches a very lucky burst of sunshine as it climbs Wittersham Bank en route to Tenterden. KESR

Northiam station was for 10 years the terminus of the revived line and has extensive parking facilities and a buffet. Parking is encouraged here for a trip to Bodiam as there are no parking facilities at the current terminus.

The village seen on the other side of the valley is Newenden, Northiam being a mile up the hill in the other direction. On its outskirts is Great Dixter, a marvellous medieval house restored by Sir Edward Lutyens and surrounded by magnificent gardens.

The next three miles see the railway sweep up the valley between the flood plain and the rich farmland on the hillsides, demonstrating Stephens' skills. As you look ahead to your right, you will see nestled under the hill the magnificent medieval castle at Bodiam that was built to defend the highest navigable point of the Rother.

The trains pass through fields that were once covered with the typical hop gardens that brought so much traffic, and finally terminate in the immaculately-restored Bodiam station, so characteristic of the light railway as built by Stephens.

Today the station building houses a booking office and seasonal gift and refreshment outlet. Across the yard are visitor toilets, housed in a building constructed in the style of a period coal merchant office. Adjacent is a waiting room which houses memorabilia from the hop-picking era with which Bodiam station was so associated.

At the rear of the station reconstructed hoppers' huts are complemented by a small hop garden.

Bodiam Castle is a 10-minute walk away across the valley. Visitors can step back in history as they explore the impressive battlements and towers, which offer breath-taking views across the countryside.

Edwardian postcard of Bodiam Castle, a choice destination for KESR passengers. ROBIN JONES COLLECTION

Bodiam Castle. 3

The last Sheppey Light Railway train at Leysdown-on-Sea on December 2, 190. CSRM

The two restored coaches which ran on the Sheppey Light Railway are now in service on the Isle of Wight Steam Railway. IOWSR

SHEPPEY LIGHT RAILWAY

The next rural backwater to benefit from a Colonel Stephens light railway was the Isle of Sheppey off the north coast of Kent, but it was soon 'swallowed up' by one of the big main line companies.

Situated just 42 minutes from central London, Sheppey – which takes its name from the Old English term for 'sheep island' – could hardly be any more different in character to the capital. Much of it is very sparsely populated marshy land heavily bisected by inlets and drainage ditches and largely used for grazing. Indeed, historically it comprised three islands: Sheppey itself, the Isle of Harty to the south east and the Isle of Elmley; but over time the channels dividing them silted up to make one continuous island.

Leysdown-on-Sea was a small coastal hamlet up to late Victorian times. Plans were laid to link it to the railway network in 1896 and Stephens was chosen by promoter the Peterson Syndicate to engineer a standard gauge light railway which was authorised on April 3, 1899.

The Sheppey Light Railway ran for nine miles from Queenborough on the London Chatham & Dover Railway's Sheerness branch to Leysdown. A single-track line, it had only one passing loop, at the intermediate station of Eastchurch. Other stations were at Sheerness East, East Minster-on-Sea and Minster-on-Sea.

While he engineered the line, it never became part of Stephens' empire. From its opening on August 1, 1901, it was worked by the South Eastern & Chatham Railway (SECR), which added halts at

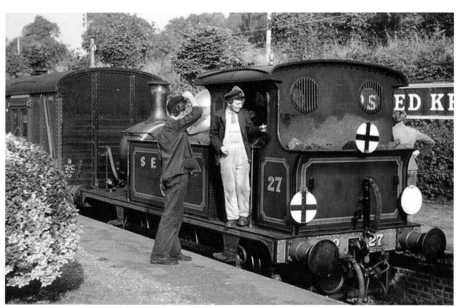

SECR P2 0-6-0T was built at Ashford Works in 1910 and entered traffic at Sheerness shed for use on the Sheppey Light Railway on February 19 that year. It is part of the Bluebell Railway fleet and is seen at Horsted Keynes in 1972. It last steamed two years later and is awaiting restoration. Half of the eight-strong P2 class survive in preservation. ROBIN WEBSTER*

Brambledown and Harty Road after it bought the line outright in 1905. While it had many of the characteristics of a Stephens light railway, he told his father "I have not much to do with the (traffic) arrangements as I am only Engineer."

As first planned, the railway was to run along a shorter 7¾-mile route to the

south, but local people complained that they would be missed out, and so the western section was moved further to the north in order to serve more people.

Following the building of the line, there were visions of turning Leysdown-on-Sea into a large seaside resort with hotels. And being run by a 'big' railway

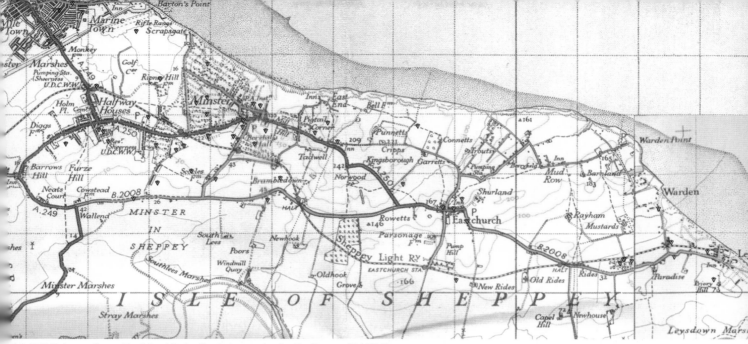

A 1940 Ordnance Survey Provisional Series One Inch map showing the Sheppey Light Railway.

meant that the new line quickly lost much of its light railway character.

At the start, the SECR used standard locomotives and stock to run the line, but found that the traffic was too light to justify them.

Two petrol-engined railcars were trialled in 1904, and while one of them, a 16-seater, proved to be up to the mark, in those days in remote Sheppey, a motor mechanic could not be found to maintain it, and so the experiment was aborted. Ironically, the UK's first aircraft factory was built in Leysdown in 1909 by the Short Brothers, and on May 2 that

locomotive steam engine components were scrapped but the carriage portions were linked in pairs via a shared bogie, and so they remained in use on the Sheppey line – but conventionally hauled by steam locomotives in the tried-and-tested manner.

Furthermore, because the steam railmotors had insufficient power to pull freight wagons, the SECR bought 'Terrier' 0-6-0T No. 54 *Waddon* second-hand from close rival, the London Brighton & South Coast Railway. Renumbered No. 751 by the SECR and nicknamed 'The

The terminus at Leysdown-on-Sea was provided with Colonel Stephens' standard corrugated iron building. ROBIN JONES COLLECTION

SHEPPEY LIGHT RAILWAY STATION, LEYSDOWN

London, Chatham & Dover Railway 2-4-0T No.518 *Sondes* being prepared by its crew in the bay platform at Queenborough station. This class of six locomotives designed by William Martley was built in 1865 and passed to the South Eastern & Chatham Railway in 1899. All were withdrawn in 1909. CSRM

...arty Road Halt was typical of the low-platformed ...tation on the Sheppey Light Railway. CSRM

...ear, John Moore-Brabazon became the ...rst resident British citizen to make a ...ecognised powered heavier-than-air ...ight in the UK flying from the Aero ...lub's grounds at Leysdown in his Voisin ...iplane Bird of Passage.

Then two steam railmotors – a ...endy rail transport development of the ...dwardian times in which a small steam ...ngine was permanently coupled to a car- ...age portion and fitted so that they train ...ould be driven from a cab at the rear ...d – were bought by the SECR in 1905, ...e for the Sheppey line and one for the ...ually remote Hundred of Hoo branch ...the opposite side of the Medway estu- ...y. Another six were purchased in 1906 ...r use on other lightly-used services, and ...ey remained in traffic until the outbreak ...the First World War. Withdrawn, the

One of the South Eastern & Chatham Railway steam railmotors which ran on the line. CSRM

STEAM RAIL CAR.
SOUTH EASTERN & CHATHAM RAILWAY.

R1 0-4-4T No. 31705 heads the final train at Queenborough on December 2, 1950, the last day of operation of the Shppey Light Railway. The R class was designed by James Stirling as a new class, and 25 were built at Ashford Works between 1888-98. The last was withdrawn in 1960. CSRM

wagon superintendent from 1899 to 1913, designed the P class 0-6-0Ts as an attempt to update the 'Terriers' with the Sheppey Light Railway line in mind. While the P2s were used on the line for several decades, they were found to be underpowered, having only 73% as much tractive effort as 'Terriers', and were later reallocated to shunting and station pilot duties.

At first, the light railway was reasonably successful, but like others of the same ilk lost out to road competition.

Little Tich,' after Harry Relph, a leading comedy actor of the day. Unfortunately, water supplies on the railway were inadequate for a small tank and *Waddon* had been moved away by 1910.

Jumping a few decades ahead here, *Waddon* is still with us today, albeit at Exporail, the Canadian Railway Museum in Montreal to which it was exported in

1963 to illustrate the differences between European and North-American locomotives. In 2003, the Bluebell Railway had a bid to repatriate it rebuffed by the museum. It was recently cosmetically restored by a group of Canadian enthusiasts of UK origin.

Meanwhile in 1910, Harry Wainwright, the SECR locomotive, carriage and

Sheppey Light Railway veteran 'Terrier' No. 70 *Waddon* in exile at Exporail, the Canadian Railway Museum in Montreal, in 2019. DENNIS JARVIS*

East Minster station with the local store next to the level crossing. CSRM

The side extension to the Costcutter store occupies the site of the former East Minster station. NIGEL COX*

In British Railways days, London, Chatham & Dover Railway Kirtley R1 0-4-4Ts Nos. 31698 and 31705 were in use on the line. However, the nationalised railway was not prepared to stand the mounting losses and the line closed on December 2, 1950.

Leysdown did not mushroom with large hotels as had been hoped when the railway first opened, but today has one of the largest concentrations of holiday parks in Kent, with many visitors coming from London. It is well known for its family amusement arcades adjacent to the sea. However, the loss of the railway left the village with only one road in. The B2231 has regular bus services providing the sole public transport links to the rest of Sheppey and the mainland.

SHEPPEY COACHES RUNNING TODAY

Two carriages that saw service on the line, London, Chatham & Dover Railway six-wheeled saloon brake third No. 4112 No. 20 and six-wheeled saloon composite No. 6369, have survived into preservation and have been restored to running order.

In 1924, after the Isle of Wight Railway was absorbed into Southern Railway ownership, the pair were sent to Lancing Works in Sussex for conversion to push-pull operation and both lost their centre pair of wheels, No. 4112 becoming a push-pull driving trailer.

Together the set, No. 484, worked mainly on the Merstone-Ventnor West branch although it occasionally ran on the Freshwater and Bembridge lines.

The set was withdrawn in 1938 and both carriage bodies sold out of service to become bungalows, No. 4112 at Gurnard Marsh and No. 6369 at Newtown. Both bodies were eventually acquired by the Isle of Wight Steam Railway and returned to service, mounted on Southern Railway parcels van underframes. Set No. 484 is now in regular passenger service.

The coast at Leysdown-on-Sea. ROBIN JONES

Chapter 6

PLYMOUTH, DEVONPORT & SOUTH WESTERN JUNCTION RAILWAY

Unique among the Colonel Stephens lines, part of his Callington branch in Cornwa is still used by passenger trains today as part of the national network.

The Tamar, Kit Hill and Callington Railway Company was formed in 1862 to build a line from the tin, copper and arsenic mines and quarries around Callington in east Cornwall to take ore and stone to be loaded on to barges on the quays on the River Tamar at Calstock.

Building work on the railway began the following year, but was stopped in 1866 when the company ran into financial problems.

A new Callington and Calstock Railway was formed to take over the project in 1869, and two years later the railway, which was built to 3ft 6in gauge,

was retitled the East Cornwall Mineral Railway. Officially opened on May 7, 18 some parts of it had already seen traffic for up to five years before.

The line ran from Kelly Bray, a mile north of the town of Callington, for nea eight miles to Calstock, where an 800ft long rope-worked incline dropped dow

The magnificent Calstock viaduct which was completed under the supervision of Colonel Stephens to link the Callington branch to the Plymouth, Devonport & South Western Junction Railway main line. MARK AC PHOTOS*

y around 350ft to reach the quays. It had ublic goods depots at Kelly Bray, Monks orner, Cox's Park, Drakewalls and on 'alstock Quay, as well as several private dings serving industrial concerns en ute.

Two Neilson 04-0STs dating from 1871 ere bought to work the line.

At first, the mineral railway was a huge uccess, and plans were drawn up to con-ct it to the national rail network.

The London & South Western Railway, hich had emerged as a major rival of the

Great Western Railway, had long sought to build its own line to Plymouth.

Whereas the South Devon Railway (later GWR), as engineered by Isambard Kingdom Brunel, built a nature-defying route from Exeter which spectacularly hugged the cliffs around Dawlish and Teignmouth before climbing a series of banks to the south of Dartmoor, the LSWR sought a route to the north of the moor from Exeter through Okehampton. The LSWR encouraged the friendly Devon & Cornwall Railway Company to

build the line then took over this smaller company on January 1, 1872.

However, while Brunel's route served a succession of towns, the rival one favoured by the LSWR had difficult, sparsely-populated terrain to cross. The route at first did not reach Plymouth, but in 1876 ended up at a terminus at Lydford next to the South Devon Railway's station on its Launceston via Tavistock to Marsh Mills branch.

The LSWR's trains could still reach Plymouth, but only by way of obtaining

One of the two Neilson 0-4-0STs built for the East Cornwall Mineral Railway. TAMAR BELLE HERITAGE CENTRE

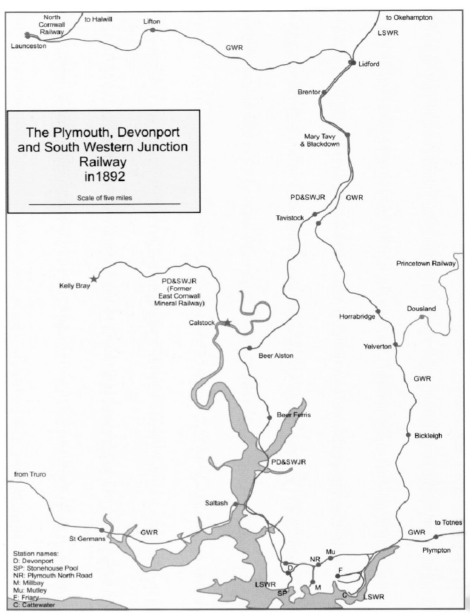

The Plymouth, Devonport and South Western Junction Railway in 1892

Scale of five miles

Station names:
D: Devonport
SP: Stonehouse Pool
NR: Plymouth North Road
M: Millbay
Mu: Mutley
F: Friary
C: Cattewater

The Plymouth, Devonport & South Western Junction Railway in 1892, with the East Cornwall Mineral Railway still a separate identity. AFTERBRUNEL*

running powers over the Marsh Mills branch. However, it still desperately wanted independent access to the great naval city.

On August 25, 1883, the Plymouth, Devonport & South Western Junction Railway (PD&SWJR) was authorised to build new independent line in Plymouth linking the city's Friary and Devonport stations, and with a large central Plymouth station east of Tavistock Road, plus a link from Devonport to Lydford. An agreement was reached with the LSWR for it to operate the line in exchange for 50% of gross receipts.

Goods traffic over the new line started on May 12, 1890, and passenger traffic on June 1. The following year the East Cornwall Minerals Railway was purchased by the PD&SWJR with the aim of extending it eastwards across the River Tamar to a new junction at Bere Alston station.

In March 1898, the secretary of the mineral railway was asked to look into the possibility of building a light railway to 3ft 6in gauge from Bere Alston to Calstock, and the statutory powers for this were obtained in 1900.

The preliminary work for this upgrade was carried out by Galbraith & Church, which had long been the consulting engineers to both the LSWR and the PD&SWJR. The firms drew up specifications for a great 12-arch viaduct which would span the Tamar at Calstock and which would physically connect both lines.

Realising that they were short of light railway expertise, in February 1904 the engineers asked the board of the PD&SWJR to seek the involvement of a master in that particular field: Holman F Stephens.

THE CALLINGTON BRANCH
The PD&SWJR directors accepted Stephens as a representative of Galbraith & Church and he worked on the project for the next six years.

An order was obtained for the narrow gauge line to be converted to standard gauge in 1905, and this particular job took only two days. It was upgraded to carry passenger trains, with new stations then being built to replace the old mineral depots.

Stephens appears to have taken on the major responsibility for not only building the branch but also operating it.

The new extension was known officially as the Bere Alston & Calstock Light Railway, but colloquially was referred to as the Calstock Light Railway, a name which was subsequently applied to the entire Callington branch, which opened on March 2, 1908.

The viaduct, which was built from concrete blocks and stands 120ft above river level, took three years to build. There were difficulties with two of the river piers and building some of the arches, each of which has a 60ft span, but today it remains one of the biggest and most dramatic examples of engineering on any Stephens line.

Despite being perfectly serviceable, the old rope-worked incline which reached the quay below the magnificent new viaduct was superseded by a steam-driven vertical wagon hoist on

the Calstock side. It was designed by Galbraith & Church rather than Stephens and could raise and lower wagons to the quays 113ft below. As such it was one of the highest lifts in the country and it was linked to the station goods yard by a second parallel steel stub viaduct.

A short section of the 3ft 6in gauge line was kept to serve a lime kiln. The new stations of the line were typical Stephens style, as was much of the rest of the infrastructure.

However, the LSWR refused to work the branch and therefore Stephens was asked to obtain three second-hand LSWR locomotives along with carriages and wagons to provide services. The LSWR had no engines to sell, so in 1906 Stephens was asked to source three new ones instead. These were built by Hawthorn Leslie and delivered in late 1907.

No. 3, an 0-6-0T, was named *A.S. Harris* while Nos. 4 and 5, 0-6-2Ts, were named *Earl of Mount Edgcumbe and Lord St Levan* respectively (all after PD&SWJR directors), while one of the mineral railway's old Neilson tanks was converted to a standard gauge 0-4-2T named *Kelly* and given a second life.

The LSWR sold 16 old carriages to the PD&SWJR in 1906, and wagons were purchased from RY Pickering of Wishaw the following year. However, the company found within a few years that it had ordered too much rolling stock, and sold many items off.

Fruit and flowers were an important part of branch freight and indeed were still carried by train from Calstock until the mid-1970s.

A big problem with the branch was the terminus being so far away from the town it purported to serve. Local people wanted to see the line extended from Kelly Bray to Callington itself, but the PD&SWJR insisted it would do that only if it was given the necessary land for free. In 1908, Stephens surveyed an extension from Kelly Bray into North Hill parish, and on February 11, 1909, the North Hill Light Railway Order was granted, but the extension was never built.

The branch ran as a separate concern from the PD&SWJR with Stephens appointed manager and engineer, but he could not commit to the two days a week attendance that the company required.

In June 1910, he left the company's employ, but still kept in touch. The following year he bought some ex-LSWR coaches for the Shropshire & Montgomeryshire Railway, and in 1912 he acquired the converted Neilson tank for the Selsey Tramway, where it was renamed *Hesperus*.

The PD&SWJR retained control of the branch as an independent railway until it was absorbed by the LSWR just before the Grouping of 1923, when the LSWR became part of the Southern Railway.

Afterwards, the local mining industry fell into decline and several of the private sidings on the branch were closed. The

A postcard view of Calstock station in 1908, showing the typical Holman F Stephens station building.

Calstock viaduct under construction. It was made from poured rather than pre-cast concrete. CSRM

Calstock wagon hoist was removed in 1934.

CASTLE'S DEFENCE

The nationwide, and indeed worldwide, switch from railways to road transport led to a steep decline in use of former PD&SWJR lines in the 1950s. Not only was the Callington branch a prime rural route for closure under British Railways

chairman Dr Richard Beeching's cuts of the Sixties, but his axe was also sharpened for the Southern Railway route from Exeter to Plymouth.

Part of Beeching's strategy for stemming the soaring losses made by the national rail network in the face of increasing competition from road transport and car ownership was to eliminate routes that 'doubled up'. In the south west, two main lines linked Exeter to Plymouth, and one of them had to go.

In his landmark report, The Reshaping of British Railways, which immediately sent shockwaves through the UK rail system when it was published on March 27, 1963, the Callington branch was among an encyclopaedic list of loss-making rural routes listed for closure – to widespread public dismay.

However, on December 23, 1965, Barbara Castle was appointed as the Labour government's Transport Minister. While Labour had pledged to reverse the Beeching cuts when it fought the 1964 General Election, it carried on with his closure recommendations regardless after winning power. Mrs Castle oversaw

An early postcard view of Callington station.

Plymouth, Devonport & South Western Junction Railway 0-6-2T No.5 *Lord St Leven* pulls out of Callington station. The station, a mile from the town it served, opened on March 2, 1908, as Callington Road and the following year was renamed Callington for Stoke Climsland.

A Plymouth, Devonport & South Western Junction Railway train at Callington station. CSRM

the closure of around 2050 miles of railway lines – including both routes within the Beeching plan and routes that the doctor had not proscribed.

However, her 1968 Transport Act introduced a new social factor into legislation regarding such closures, and a further 3500 miles were given the possibility of a reprieve.

Castle recognised that while many services earmarked for closure were indeed non-remunerative, as Beeching had identified, they nonetheless played a vital social role. If they closed the communities they served would suffer hardship.

While railway closures rapidly continued, Castle saved several individual routes including branch lines such as York to Harrogate, Manchester to Buxton,

Oxenholme to Windermere, Exeter to Exmouth and in Cornwall, the Looe branch and the St Ives line.

The Looe branch was saved, for example, because of the difficult winding roads serving the resort. In a similar vein, part of the Bere Alston to Callington branch was saved, because of the hilly terrain at the point where the rivers Tamar and Tavy meet and the circuitous road routes. The nearest road crossing over the Tamar is the A390 at Gunnislake, which left the railway as the quickest way of getting into Plymouth to the south.

Instead of full closure, the branch was truncated at Gunnislake. The now-closed section of line north of Gunnislake was remote from local communities and provided a relatively slow journey compared with the competing roads,

while Callington had good bus services to Saltash and Plymouth. However, the landscape denied those advantages to Gunnislake.

The line was retained as far north as Bere Alston, but lifted between there and Meldon Quarry. Goods services on the Callington branch were withdrawn on February 28, 1966, and the section from Callington to Gunnislake was closed altogether on November 7, 1966. Under the new arrangement, trains had to reverse at Bere Alston, which is still the case today.

The original Gunnislake station lay on the west side of the road bridge. In 1994 it was replaced by a new station on the east (Calstock) side which has allowed the low (12ft) bridge to be demolished.

TAMAR VALLEY LINE

The surviving part of the PD&SWJR including the Gunnislake branch is today branded as the Tamar Valley Line. Having the distinction of being the only Colonel Stephens railway to survive in passenger use as part of today's national network, it is one of the railway lines supported by the Devon and Cornwall Rail Partnership, an organisation formed in 1991 to promote railway services in the south west. The line is promoted by many means such as regular timetable and scenic line guides, as well as leaflets highlighting leisure opportunities such as walking or visiting country pubs.

The Tamar Valley rail ale trail was launched in 2004 to encourage rail travellers to visit pubs near the line. Seven are in Plymouth city centre and one in the suburb of Devonport. There are single pubs to visit at Bere Ferrers, Bere Alston and Calstock and four in Gunnislake.

The overall number of passengers travelling on the Tamar Valley line has grown by more than 50% since 2001 and Gunnislake is the busiest station on the line.

The journey from Plymouth typically takes 45 minutes. During the summer nine trains each way operate on weekdays, eight on Saturdays and six on Sundays. Connections with main line services can be made at Plymouth.

The line was designated as a community rail line in September 2005, being one of seven pilots for the Department for

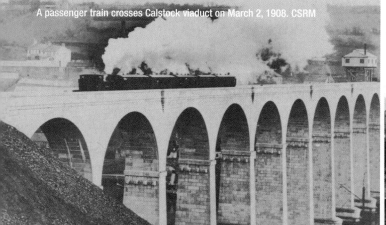

A passenger train crosses Calstock viaduct on March 2, 1908. CSRM

No. 3 *A.S. Harris* at Bere Alston station on April 7, 1919. CSRM

A postcard of Gunnislake station which was sent in 1909. CSRM

Bere Alston station in 1930.

Transport's Community Rail Development Strategy, which aims to establish the true costs and revenues for the line with an aim of improving them. It also began looking at simplifying the reversal of trains and the potential for extending the line from Bere Alston to Tavistock, making the former a junction station again, just as it had been in the Stephens era.

On March 18, 2008, Devon County Council backed a proposal by developers Kilbride Community Rail to build 750 houses in Tavistock that included reopening the 5½-mile route from Bere Alston to a new Tavistock station at a cost of £18.5 million. However, at the time of writing, no progress on any reinstatement of the line had been made.

Furthermore, there have been repeated calls for the Southern Railway route from Exeter to Plymouth to be reopened, providing an all-weather alternative to Brunel's legendary South Devon coastal route.

On the night of February 4, 2014, amid high winds and extremely rough seas, part of the sea wall at Dawlish was breached, washing away around 130ft of the wall and the ballast under the railway immediately behind, leaving the tracks suspended in mid-air like a rope bridge. Closure of the line impacted on the economies of Plymouth and its hinterland. Network Rail immediately set about repairs and the line reopened on April 4, 2014.

The disaster led many to campaign for the alternative route to be rebuilt. The Southern route remains in use between Exeter and Crediton at part of Network Rail's Tarka Line to Barnstaple, and beyond Crediton, it survives for another 15½ miles as part of the Dartmoor Railway, which runs through Sampford Courtenay and Okehampton to Meldon Quarry. Passenger services from Exeter to Okehampton survived until 1972, after which this section of the Southern route was retained to service the ballast quarry at Meldon. After the freight traffic ceased, it was reborn as a heritage railway.

Observers have argued that rebuilding the route from Meldon Quarry to Tavistock, the proposed terminus of a new 'branch' from Bere Alston, would provide a more durable route between Exeter and Plymouth that would be far less costly to maintain than the alternative through Dawlish.

Hawthorn Leslie 0-6-2T No.5 *Lord St Leven*, carrying its LSWR number 758, heads the 12.40pm Bere Alston to Callington goods near Callington on June 20, 1949. Under British Railways, the locomotive was renumbered 30758 and withdrawn in December 1956. CSRM

However, both the Government and Network Rail decided to persevere with Brunel's route. In 2018 Network Rail announced proposals to extend the sea wall farther into the English Channel at Teignmouth, realigning the railway by moving it further from the cliff and creating a space between them to prevent the line being affected by cliff subsidence or collapse. Other elements of the proposal include the improvement of the sea wall between Kennaway Tunnel and Dawlish and the installation of an avalanche shelter-style structure at Horse Cove. Government funding of £80 million to raise the sea wall south of Dawlish station by 8ft was approved in February 2019. So it seems that there is now no way back for the Southern route despite its advantages.

THE TAMAR BELLE

While the Tamar Valley Line's Bere Ferrers station was opened by the PD&SWJR on June 2, 1890, well before the coming of Stephens to the locality, and was not part of the Callington branch at any stage, it is now home to the Tamar Belle Heritage Centre, which admirably showcases the railway history of the locality, as well as providing holiday accommodation in converted coaches.

Its story begins in 1980, when enthusiast Chris Grove was working in London as a chartered surveyor. He happened to spot an advertisement in *The Times* for the auction of a station house at Bere Ferrers and drove 225 miles to buy it.

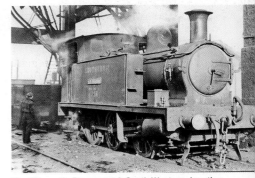

The Plymouth, Devonport & South Western Junction Railway's Hawthorn Leslie 0-6-0T No. 3 *A.S. Harris*, which had been ordered by Colonel Stephens and delivered in 1907, after the Grouping of 1923 became used as a shed pilot all over the Southern Railway system until it was withdrawn in October 1951. It is pictured at Stewarts Lane depot in London. BEN BROOKSBANK*

Labour Transport Minister Barbara Castle saved the section of the Callington branch from Bere Alston to Gunnislake.

Class 118 diesel multiple unit set comprising cars Nos. 51312 and 51327 form the 7.15pm service from the original Gunnislake station to Plymouth on July 14, 1984. PHIL RICHARDS*

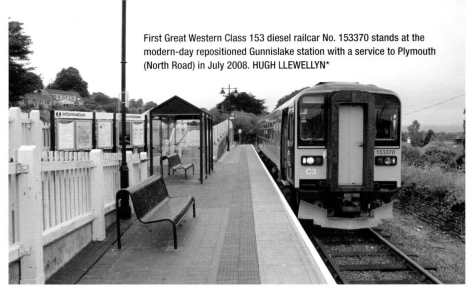

First Great Western Class 153 diesel railcar No. 153370 stands at the modern-day repositioned Gunnislake station with a service to Plymouth (North Road) in July 2008. HUGH LLEWELLYN*

RIGHT: Class 150 diesel multiple unit No. 150248 at Bere Alston station on July 16, 2017. JUSTIN & TERRY FOULGER RAILWAY PHOTOGRAPHY

Chris had spent several years working in railway site redevelopment for British Rail Property Board, and now turned that experience to good personal use. He successfully renovated and sold the stationmaster's house in the first year and then concentrated on restoring the former booking hall as a holiday home, later converting it into his own residence, moving there during the Nineties.

In 1988, he bought the redundant LSWR signalbox at Pinhoe and relocated it to Bere Ferrers, where it was installed at the end of the Tamar Valley Line platform.

On June 2, 1990, to mark the centenary of the station's opening, Chris laid a 700ft demonstration track in the former yard and borrowed diminutive ex-Port of Par Bagnall 0-4-0ST *Alfred* from the Bodmin & Wenford Railway and so returned steam to the Tamar Valley for a weekend.

However, with the track was in place, Chris felt it should be used on a more permanent basis. He bought two carriages from Norwich and converted them into a successful bed and breakfast business. There are now four carriages converted to provide a dining coach, saloon and two sleeping cars. He added three vintage Hunslet diesel shunters, and acquired a turntable from Plymouth dockyard.

A small group of enthusiast volunteers had become involved with the project under the banner of the Tamar Belle Heritage Group, and established the interpretative visitor centre.

Among its projects has been the installation of a working signalling system with 12 operational signals in a converted cattle truck, controlling three trains shuttling on the one line. It is also home to Peckett 0-6-0ST No. 1963 of 1938 *Hilda*, which was delivered new to the Plasterworks of Cafferata & Co at Newark, later British Gypsum, and preserved in December 1971. It spent many years in storage at the Great Central Railway at Loughborough before moving to Bere Ferrers in 1996.

Today, visitors to the Tamar Belle can enjoy lunch, afternoon tea or dinner in luxury Pullman style, climb aboard the guard's van, visit the signalbox and watch shunting demonstrations and inspect a treasure trove of railway relics. More details can be found at www.tamarbelle.co.uk or by telephoning 07813 360066.

These two Hunslet diesels at the Tamar Belle Heritage Centre at Bere Ferrers station on the Tamar Valley Line now carry the numbers and names of steam locomotives bought by Colonel Stephens for the Callington branch, in No. 3 *A.S. Harris* and No. 4 *Earl of Mount Edgcumbe*. MARK AC PHOTOS

Bere Ferrers station today, with the Tamar Belle Heritage Centre in the yard to the right. TAMAR BELLE HERITAGE CENTRE

One of the original works plates from *Pontyberem* recently acquired by the Gwendraeth Railway Society. STUART THOMAS

Double Fairlie Mountaineer of 1869 at Burry Port in the 1890s. The Burry Port & Gwendraeth Valley Railway was the only standard gauge line in the UK to regularly use double Fairlies. GRS

THAT LINE WITH THE LOWEST BRIDGES

The somewhat curious 'canal conversion' Burry Port & Gwendraeth Valley Railway in Carmarthenshire came into the Colonel Stephens' sphere in 1908.

Coal had been mined to the north of Llanelly for centuries, but carrying it from the hills to the nearest harbour had always proved difficult and costly.

Around 1768, Thomas Kymer had built a canal – the first of its kind in Wales – to Pwll-y-Llygod for the purpose. From the head of the canal, a wooden-railed waggonway was built to serve the pits at Carway a mile away. The line was upgraded in 1796 when John Curr introduced a plateway system, in which flat plates with an upstand for guidance carried wagons with plain as opposed to the earlier flanged wheels.

The Carmarthenshire Railway opened in 1804. It was a plateway linking coal pits near Cross Hands and ironworks to its own harbour at Llanelly. Before then, the local horse-drawn waggonway system which led to Llanelly lacked wharfage there, and so ships had to be beached to load the coal.

In 1865, at a time when moves were afoot to reopen the old Carmarthenshire Railway, the Llanelly Railway & Dock Company sought to combat this potential local competition and obtained powers to absorb Kymer's canal and build 18½ miles of new railways from Burry Port to a junction with its Mountain branch, plus a second main line to Cross Hands Colliery.

The expanded system then underwent a name change to the Kidwelly & Burry

An early 20th century view of Burry Port station. COLONEL STEPHENS SOCIETY

Port Railway Company. The following year, it merged with the Burry Port Harbour Company to become the Burry Port & Gwendreath Valley Railway (BP&GVR), the name Gwendraeth being misspelled in the authorised documents.

The canal was closed in 1868 and the new railway was laid as far as possible on the towpath. Under certain bridges the line was laid at a lower level than the towpath, necessitating short downgrades to pass beneath. However, the headroom at the overbridges was still left very restricted, leading to problems for the subsequent railway later.

The line was officially opened as far as Pontyberem on June 23, 1869, with branches to Carway opened in late 1870 and to the Star Colliery at Trimsaran in June 1872. The main line was completed to the foot of the Hirwaen Isaf incline, a mile short of Cwm Mawr, in 1870. The opening of this railway and its branches immediately brought prosperity to local mines and made the transportation of the extracted coal more efficient and less costly.

In December 1869 the BP&GVR tried out a double Fairlie locomotive named *Pioneer*, which had been constructed for a Swedish railway but had not been delivered. The trial proved very successful and the company purchased the locomotive, renaming it *Mountaineer*. A second double Fairlie was acquired soon afterwards. The double-ended type is, of course, famous today for its use on the Ffestiniog Railway.

The adjacent Gwendraeth Valleys Railway (GVR) reopened in 1872 as a standard gauge line from the GWR at Kidwelly to Mynydd-y-Garreg. In November 1866, agreement was signed for the BP&GVR to work on the GVR.

In 1880 the West of England Bank failed, with the financial knock-on effect that the BP&GVR's main customer, Pontyberem Colliery, also failed. In turn, this created a financial morass for the railway company which went in receivership in July 1881.

The main line was finally completed to Cwm Mawr in June 1886, with the ruling gradient on the extension to Cwm Mawr a phenomenal 1-in-14/15 in parts because of the canal inclines that it ran over.

The BP&GVR was a mineral-only railway and as such operated without signalling. However, excursion trains ran in the 1870s to Pontnewydd in connection with the eisteddfods held in the grounds of Glyn Abbey. By the summer of 1883, occasional free passenger excursions were run from the collieries to the seaside, probably using old converted coal wagons to carry miners and their families.

A fully-fledged workmen's service was started before the end of 1898, from Burry Port and calling at Trimsaran Road bridge at Morfa to pick up miners who had walked there from Kidwelly. When the Kidwelly branch was relaid with stronger track as far as Tycoch Junction, where the Gwendraeth Valley line connected, workmen's trains ran from Tycoch Bridge, about half a mile from the centre of Kidwelly.

The collieries at Ponthenry and Penremawr wanted to see their men taken daily to the pits as there were no houses in the locality, but because the railway was in receivership it could not invest in passenger carriages. The colliery companies agreed to each buy a coach and lease it to the railway.

In addition, a Thursday market train was run to Llanelly, mainly for the miners' wives and families. The miners paid for their travel by deduction from their wages rather than by ticket, and the families visiting the market paid a charge per parcel brought home – loopholes to bypass Board of Trade rules about commercial passenger operation, and the payment of passenger duty. Indeed, the railway company looked at upgrading its line for passenger operation in 1900, but nothing was done because its financial woes were not over.

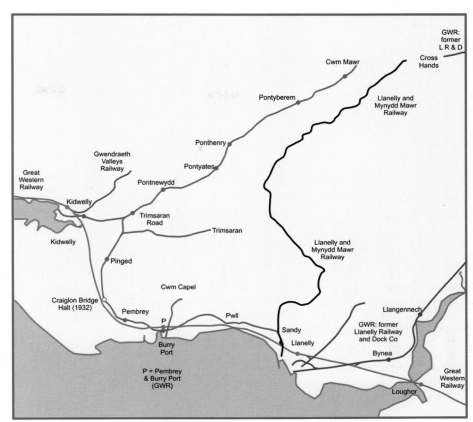

A system map of the Burry Port & Gwendraeth Valley Railway in 1909, also showing the nearby Llanelly & Mynydd Mawr Railway. AFTERBRUNEL/CREATIVE COMMONS

CALL IN HOLMAN!

However, on September 3, 1903, a locomotive collided with one of the workmen's trains. Accordingly, the Board of Trade wrote to the company three weeks later warning of the "responsibility incurred by your company in carrying persons in this manner without the proper safeguards adopted for passenger lines".

On February 16, 1904, Lt Col Yorke of the Board of Trade visited the line by the invitation of its general manager Arthur Morgan to discuss what these proper safeguards might entail, and Yorke advised that the Board of Trade "could not recognise the practice of carrying outsiders..."

Yes, it was deemed acceptable to carry workmen on the line, but not ordinary members of the general public. However, local people were demanding the operation of a public passenger service on the line, even though the railway argued that it had no money to upgrade the line for the purpose.

In March 1908, the BP&GVR agreed to look into the possibility of getting a Light Railway Order so it could rebuild the line to an official passenger-carrying standard. Its board resolved that an "engineer of experience... should be consulted."

So Holman Stephens was brought in. As was his customary approach, he sprang straight into action, and reported to the July board meeting that year. Solicitors were instructed to apply

for a Light Railway Order covering the route from Burry Port to Pontyberem, plus the branch to Ty Coch. New heavier rails were ordered together with a new locomotive and signalling equipment. Ten secondhand coaches were obtained from the Metropolitan Railway.

The Light Railway Order was confirmed by the Board of Trade on June 30, 1909 and the fully-fledged passenger service began on August 2, 1909. Public stations were at Burry Port (immediately south of the GWR's Pembrey & Burry Port station), Pembrey, Pinged, Trimsaran Road, Pontnewydd (renamed Glyn Abbey in 1910), Pontyates, Ponthenry station and Pontyberem.

The workmen's trains on the main line became regular service trains, but the Ponthenry and Pentremawr Colliery halts were not shown in the public timetable, and only certain trains stopped there. The halt at Trimsaran Road became a regular stopping place, and additional halts were opened to serve other collieries at Trimsaran Junction and Carway Colliery Sidings between Glyn Abbey and Pontyates.

The railway had come under pressure from local residents to extend the passenger services all the way to Cwmmawr, but deferred making a decision until June 1910 after consulting Stephens.

Plans were drawn up by March 1911 and another Light Railway Order was applied for. It was reported that Stephens

Stephens' station at Pontyates after his reconstruction of the line. COLONEL STEPHENS SOCIETY

was far from enthusiastic about the extension however, as substantial new earthworks were required to ease the abovementioned harsh gradient to 1-in-40. A quarter-mile-long cutting was dug and 1000 yards of embankment raised 30ft above the original trackbed.

Stephens had suggested that Cwmmawr could have instead been served by building a line running north to the LNWR at Llanatheney, which had been authorised in 1881 but never built, and keeping the existing line for coal traffic. However, his idea was not accepted, perhaps because linking the BP&GVR to the LNWR would have upset the GWR.

The Light Railway Order was confirmed by the Board of Trade on October 4, 1911, and three former London & South Western Railway six-wheel coaches were obtained and converted to four-wheelers.

Passenger services to Cwmmawr started on January 29, 1913. Eleven days earlier, Stephens wrote that he was "finishing my work" on the BP&GVR and praised the line's engineer John Eager who had worked under him on the reconstruction of the line for five years.

So Stephens left the BP&GVR on a firm footing in engineering terms.

LIFE AFTER STEPHENS

The BP&GVR would, however, remain handicapped by the restricted loading gauge which resulted from it having been built on the course of a canal, and the low bridges were never to be raised.

The company briefly considered rebuilding it again in 1919 but took no action. At the time, the line was carrying 187,000 passengers and 355 miners each year, and the company was paying a 10% dividend to shareholders.

However, as a port, Burry Port was in decline, with collieries preferring Swansea Docks where larger ships and mechanical handling facilities allowed

A sepia postcard view of Burry Port station.

coal could be dealt with more efficiently. Also, the silting of the Gwendraeth estuary led to the little quay at Kidwelly being much less used after 1920, and the last traffic to use it before closure in October 1929 was understood to be carrying roadstone. The branch to the quay was lifted in 1933.

The Railways Act 1921 led to most of Britain's railways being 'grouped' into four large concerns. The Ministry of Transport offered to leave the BP&GVR independent as a locally-managed railway, but its directors had already been considering a sale to the GWR, which duly absorbed it from July 1, 1922.

With passenger services making a loss thanks to declining numbers in the face of bus competition, British Railways ran its last passenger trains over the line on Saturday, September 19, 1953.The line was retained for freight, but its branches closed with the demise of the deep mines.

Diesels were introduced on the BP&GVR section on October 4, 1965, in the form of two D2000 class (later Class 03) shunters which were modified to work together in multiple, and soon a third was used to bank the trains up the steep gradients. On the downhill journey the three locomotives hauled the train. The cabs were cut down to pass under the low bridges on the line. Class 03s were used because of the frequent flooding on part of the line which would interfere with the low-slung auxiliary equipment on the more powerful Class 08s, but in June 1984 the affected section of line was closed and so three 08s were modified to lower the profile for the low bridges and were designated Class 08/9. The 0-8s were redesigned and modified at Landor Traction Maintenance Depot in Swansea between 1985-87 by being given

headlights and cut-down bodywork line with overall height reduced to 11ft 10in for use on the freight line to Cwmmawr.

The last train to Cwmmawr ran on Friday, March 29, 1996, with closure of this remaining section of the BP&GVR main line taking place on April 1, 1996. While Coed Bach continued to be fed by road, rail traffic remained over the short distance from there to Kidwelly yard. However, this surviving section finally closed on March 23, 1998.

THE HERITAGE ERA

In the wake of the closure, the line came to the attention of the preservation/revivalist movement. May 2002 saw a new Burry Port and Gwendraeth Valley Railway Co Ltd incorporated with a view to reviving the line. Enthusiasts drew up an initial scheme which involved regauging the mothballed line to accommodate continental and American rolling stock.

Metre gauge was identified for the revival of the route because of the notorious low bridges which required the use of locomotives with cut-down cabs like the latter-day Class 08/9s. Indeed, talks between representatives of the new company and the Portuguese national railway authorities about the acquisition of at least five redundant steam and diesel locomotives and nine carriages began.

However, the revival scheme under the banner of the Gwendraeth Railway Society (GRS) has long since changed direction. As the time of writing, the aim is now to develop the UK's first velo-rail (railbike) line with a supporting standard gauge heritage railway visitor attraction. Complex discussions have been completed to agree the terms of a lease for 99 years for a nominal rent to include branch and associated

land and sidings. Final legal agreements are in preparation pending Network Rail and rail regulatory bodies completing the final industry sign off.

Several strategies to acquire or build sufficient numbers of high-quality velo-rail vehicles have been examined. Options include purchase of an initial batch from existing suppliers in Europe or the Far East or the currently preferred option to design and build UK specific vehicles adapted for local climatic conditions (in this case, mainly rain). A third option is a scheme to recover and reuse components from scrap bicycles in collaboration with local third sector groups and training providers to produce a sustainable supply of velo-rails for the project.

With regard to the classic heritage railway side of the project, the company now has a fleet of three locomotives. The society bought the sole-surviving original BP&GVR steam locomotive, Avonside 0-6-0ST No. 1421 of 1900 *Pontyberem* from the Great Western Society (GWS) in 2009 and moved it to the Pontypool & Blaenavon Railway.

Pontyberem had been purchased new by the BP&GVR to replace the aging double Fairlies *Mountaineer* and *Victoria* which had operated the route for most of the previous 30 years almost since the time of the canal conversion in the mid 1860s. *Pontyberem* was sold into colliery service in 1914 where it survived at Mountain Ash and Penrynkeiber until preserved by the GWS and moved into storage at Didcot.

Pontyberem was followed there several months later by *Swindon*, 1960-built Class 03 No. 03141, one of the batch that also had cabs reduced in height to work on the BP&GVR. It is one of six surviving Class 03 veterans of the line.

Burry port station with a variety of carriages on July 28, 1947. COLONEL STEPHENS MUSEUM

Avonside 0-6-0ST No.1421 of 1900 Burry Port & Gwendraeth Valley Railway No. 2 *Pontyberem* (rebuilt 1953 as No.1875), NCB No.11, at Penrikyber Colliery shed in October 1968. This locomotive and Barclay 0-6-0ST No.2074 of 1958 *Penrikyber No.1* worked the yard of this colliery until 1968 when one diesel shunter replaced them. It was decided to keep one of them as standby and *Pontyberem* was chosen in favour of its partner which was just a decade old. It was withdrawn in 1970, and is now at the Pontypool & Blaenavon Railway awaiting eventual restoration for re-use on its original line. HUGH LLEWELLYN/CREATIVE COMMONS

After withdrawal in 1985 the locomotive was bought for preservation before being acquired by Cotswold Rail in 2000. In 2002 it moved to the Dean Forest Railway and was sold in 2005 to a member of the revivalist group. It was then moved to the now-closed Swansea Vale Railway for storage. Little work was done on the locomotive there due to vandalism problems.

In 2020, the revivalists bought No. 08995, one of the three surviving Class 08/9 shunters with cut-down cabs, from the North Dorset Railway at Shillingstone station in Dorset, which bought it for restoration at auction in 2015 after it was declared surplus by DB Schenker.

However, it became increasingly apparent to the trustees of the Shillingstone heritage venue that the increasing cost and complex practicalities of restoring No. 08995 were no longer realistically within the means of their charity. A fundraising and part owners' group was proposed and

The Velorail De Larzac in France – an example of the type of velo-rail operation proposed for the Gwendraeth Valley. What would Colonel Stephens have made of such an adaptation for one of 'his' former railways? STUART THOMAS

Class 08/9 shunter No. 08995, which was modified for use on the Burry Port & Gwendraeth Valley Railway in its latter-day British Rail era, has been bought by the line's revivalists. NORTH DORSET RAILWAY

raised £10,700, but much more money would have been required to complete the restoration and deliver it to Shillingstone.

Rather than continue to tie up funds in the project, the trustees decided to sell it and replace it with the smaller but fully working Hudswell Clarke 0-6-0DM D1166 of 1959 *Ashdown*, which had been restored by Andrew Briddon at Peak Rail and which was deemed better suited to Shillingstone's current needs and capabilities.

The acquisition means that the BP&GVR revivalists' entire collection of three locomotives are veterans of the line they intend to restore.

Society members have been planning the major overhaul of No. 08995 with a view to returning the working locomotive to the Gwendraeth Valley in time for the

The Burry Port storm water culvert which was formed using the boiler barrels from double Fairlie *Mountaineer*. The Gwendraeth Railway Society hopes to extract the barrels to create a static replica of the original locomotive. STUART THOMAS

Heavy vegetation cleared between Pontyates and Pont Newydd in early 2020. GRS

official launch of the project. Before then, they will focus their attention on completing the restoration of the smaller No. 03141, which will need to be available to undertake the refurbishment of sections of the route.

The group is progressing steadily with restoring *Pontyberem* to its original condition. One of the locomotive's original Avonside works plates appeared at auction and has now been reunited with the locomotive. Another lucky find was of a pair of missing eccentric rods from the locomotive which had been mistaken for GWR items and are now also back with *Ponyberem*. The society has long-term plans to add a fourth former BP&GVR locomotive, even though it will be for static display only.

In spring 2004, society members rediscovered the boiler barrels of Double Fairlie 0-4-4-0T *Mountaineer*, which for over a century had been used as a water culvert in Burry Port. It is planned to recover the barrels as the basis of a full-scale static replica of this prototype locomotive, the remains of which make it the world's oldest surviving Fairlie.

The society's first phase of restoring the route is from Kidwelly (on land adjacent to the main line junction) to Pontyates, with intermediate station halts at Trimsaren Road and Pont Newydd/ Glyn Abbey, giving a total distance of around five miles. The total distance of all planned restoration phases to Cwm Mawr via Pontyberem and Pont Henri is nine miles.

If all goes according to plan, the Burry Port & Gwendreath Railway will join the elite set of former Colonel Stephens lines that are now part of Britain's proud heritage railway portfolio of lines.

The refurbished level crossing gates and new station fencing at Pontyates. GRS

Chapter 8

The Ford two-car railcar set at Kinnerley. CSRM

THE SHROPSHIRE & MONTGOMERYSHIRE LIGHT RAILWAY

The Potteries, Shrewsbury & North Wales Railway has been described as "the railway that refused to die" as from the start it struggled to cover costs. Holman F Stephens revived it after the latest of several closures – but even his economy measures could not make it pay.

Shropshire & Montgomeryshire Railway No.1 *Gazelle* with trailer carriage No.16 in platform by the lever frame cabin, at Kinnerley on August 8, 1926. One of the smallest steam locomotives ever built for standard gauge, *Gazelle* was constructed in 1893 by Alfred Dodman & Co at King's Lynn as a 2-2-2WT to a design produced by S Stone of the Great Eastern Railway. Its first owner was William Burkitt, an amateur locomotive enthusiast who was twice mayor of King's Lynn. He had private running rights over the Midland & Great Northern and Great Eastern Railways and he used *Gazelle* on his business trips as a seed and corn dealer. In 1910 it was sold to Sheffield dealer T W Ward who resold it to Holman Stephens the following year, when W G Bagnall Ltd rebuilt it as 0-4-2WT and fitted an enclosed cab. CSRM

The railway building age of the 19th century inevitably threw up many speculative schemes where the business case was found to be far less than sound. Indeed, historians have argued with much justification that there were many

railways which should never have been built.

A classic case of a railway running from 'somewhere to nowhere' was the Potteries, Shrewsbury & North Wales Railway (PS&NWR) which, when it

opened in 1866, became infamous as most expensive non-metropolitan railway then built.

Its complicated origins were symptomatic of an era in which hundreds of small companies sprang up and built

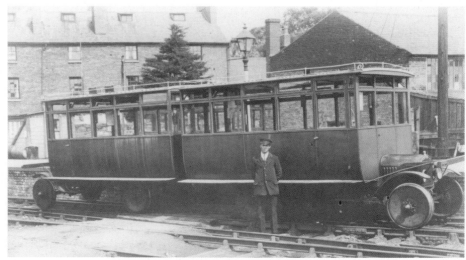

The Ford two-car railcar set, with posed driver, at Shrewsbury Abbey Foregate station. CSRM

A Potteries, Shrewsbury and North Wales Railway train at Abbey Foregate station some time between 1872-74 is headed by an 1847-built LNWR Bury, Curtis and Kennedy 0-4-2. HAROLD DALSTON/ THE RAILWAY MAGAZINE

Nantmawr

Porth

Blodwel Junction

tiny branch lines, backed by private speculators. No fewer than nine Acts of Parliament were obtained between 1862 and 1866, paving the way for its construction.

The West Shropshire Mineral Railway obtained three Acts relating to a main line between Yockleton, on the Shrewsbury & Welshpool Railway (SWR), and Llanymynech, on the Oswestry & Newtown Railway, in 1862-4. That was subsumed into the Shrewsbury & North Wales Railway (SNWR) in 1864, the SNWR obtaining three Acts by 1866 and being realigned to connect with the SWR at Hookagate in the process. In 1865, after several attempts to penetrate the Potteries towns, the Shrewsbury & Potteries Junction Railway obtained an Act to connect Shrewsbury with Market Drayton, linking the SNWR with the North Staffordshire Railway. The SNWR obtained another Act in 1866 before amalgamating with the SPJR to become the PS&NWR on the same day.

The aim of the PS&NWR, which was funded by the North Staffordshire Railway (locally known as the 'Potts Line') was to build a line from the Potteries, via Market Drayton, to quarries at Nantmawr and Criggion over the Welsh border. It was also intended to carry passengers but it never managed to penetrate the Potteries. What made the line's backers think hordes of passengers would want to travel the 18 miles from Shrewsbury to the small village of Llanymynech near Oswestry, or maybe stop off at a plethora of stations in the middle of nowhere, remains a mystery.

Yet the Potts Line was built – and to double track too – at inflated prices by contractor Richard France, who then went bankrupt. The scheme suffered a setback early on when the company was refused permission to run trains into Shrewsbury General station, meaning that the Potts Line would have to operate in isolation from the rest of the rail network.

It built its terminus at Abbey Foregate, opposite Shrewsbury's Abbey Church, standing on the site of the former monastery's refectory. Indeed, the station was the only one on the line to have a ladies' toilet.

Leaving Shrewsbury in a south-easterly direction, with a station at West Meole Brace, it headed out into lightly-populated farmland and areas that were prone to periodic heavy flooding. Its biggest engineering feat was the twin track viaduct over the River Severn at Shrawardine.

The Potts Line opened on August 13, 1866, when large numbers of passengers travelled from Abbey Foregate to explore Llanymynech. However, the novelty quickly wore off as far as the

public was concerned, to the extent that the company was plunged into financial difficulties. Debt collectors even seized a train at Abbey Foregate. It was eventually allowed to leave, but only with a bailiff on board. He waited in a stationary coach for a few minutes, but then looked out of the window to see the rest of the train disappear into the distance without him. He was eventually given the explanation that a coupling chain had broken by accident, leaving his coach behind.

A receiver was appointed and the company ceased running trains on December 21, 1866. It sold off some of its assets to satisfy creditors.

The line reopened in December 1868 and branches to Criggion and Llanyblodwel, on the Nantmawr freight branch, were formally opened for passengers in June 1871 and 1872. The Criggion branch was primarily used for transporting stone from the quarry at the foot of the Breidden Hills, and its passenger stations were extremely basic wooden affairs.

The main line was probably singled between Ford and Llanymynech in 1868-9, and between Shrewsbury and Ford in 1875.

Following a complaint to the Board of Trade concerning the condition of the Melverley river bridge on the Criggion branch, the board inspected the railway and found numerous track defects. Indeed, the condition of the track had become so bad that a 25mph speed limit was imposed all along the line. The company had neither the money nor the will to carry out repairs and the railway was abandoned on June 22, 1880.

Most of the stone traffic was continued after the Llanymynech to Nantmawr branch was leased to the Cambrian Railways in June 1880. The Potteries, Shrewsbury & North Wales Railway (Winding Up) Act was obtained in 1881, but was passed only on the proviso that the closed railway was left intact.

After the suspension of services in June 1880, Cambrian Railways (CR) came to an agreement to maintain the stunted Nantmawr branch.

On April 11, 1894, the CR agreed to build a half-mile deviation from its own Llanfyllin branch to join the Nantmawr line at Wern. The Nantmawr branch reopened for quarry traffic as a CR subsidiary on January 1, 1896 and the deviation followed on January 27. A lease for 99 years followed on April 12, 1900, with the CR paying half, the other 50% coming from the Tanat Valley Light Railway, which opened on January 5, 1904.

After the 1880 closure, the entire Potts Line became derelict, but a new company called Shropshire Railways was formed by statute in 1888 to take over the moribund route, with the intention of

The Potteries, Shrewsbury & North Wales Railway in Edwardian times, with (inset), the Nantmawr quarry branch.

The entrance to Shrewsbury Abbey Foregate station, the main headquarters for the Shropshire & Montgomery Light Railway, and before then also for the Potteries, Shrewsbury & North Wales Railway. Colonel Stephens also ran the Snailbeach and District Light Railway (see Chapter 12) from it. SHREWSBURY RAILWAY HERITAGE TRUST

extending it deeper into north Wales, as the original promoters had intended.

This company began relaying the track in 1891, but fell out several times with its potential contractors and its financiers. Accordingly, reconstruction work ceased the same year, and in 1895 the scheme finally collapsed when a fundraising prospectus failed to mention that the company was in receivership. Again, the Potts Line went to sleep for several years,

and in 1902 the wooden viaduct over the Severn at Melverley collapsed into the river.

THE STEPHENS REVIVAL

On December 20, 1906, just weeks after the board of directors considered selling off the rails, financier J H Whadcoat, who had assumed control of Shropshire Railways, met Holman F Stephens at Shrewsbury.

The approach had come from Stephens, who had taken an interest in the derelict line – but what part of the phrase 'this is a dead duck' did he not understand? He had decided that the Potts Line was not dead, but sleeping.

Following a complex series of negotiations, Whadcote and his family gave or sold their holdings in Shropshire Railways to Stephens and his associates under the banner of the Severn Syndicate of July 15, 1909, allowing the company to stay in existence.

With the backing of local councils, Stephens formed a new operating company, at first named the North Shropshire Railway but soon changed to the Shropshire & Montgomeryshire Light Railway. Leasing the Potts Line from Shropshire Railways, it obtained a Light Railway Order in February 1909, and rebuilding the line from the Llanymynech end began in late 1910.

Stephens reconstructed the line economically using the original infrastructure wherever possible. Yet again all the sleepers on the line were replaced, the stricken Melverley Viaduct was rebuilt and due to lack of space at Abbey Foregate, the locomotive centre was moved to Kinnerley.

Traffic remained at a low level but Stephens was at least able to keep costs down by bringing in a fleet of assorted second-hand locomotives and carriages

Opening day for the Shropshire & Montgomeryshire Railway with the mayor addressing the crowds at Shrewsbury Abbey Foregate station on April 13, 1911. CSRM

A freight working steams through Kinnerley Junction station, with a pump trolley next to the water column. CSRM

The first locomotive he bought was the diminutive 2-2-2T *Gazelle*, nicknamed the 'Coffee Pot' and which at first served as an inspection locomotive and then as a service locomotive on the Criggion branch.

The railway ordered two new 0-6-2Ts named *Pyramus* and *Thisbe* from Hawthorn Leslie. These were not successful, and were sold to the Government in 1916.

Early arrivals also included Manning Wardle 0-6-0ST *Morous* and Hudswell Clarke 0-6-0ST *Walton Park*. The mainstay of Stephens' reborn railway then became three former LSWR 'Ilfracombe Goods' 0-6-0s.
Three LBSCR 'Terrier' 0-6-0Ts, No. 681 *Beulah*, No. 638 *Millwall* and No. 683 *Earlswood*, which became *Hecate*, *Dido* and *Daphne* respectively, were bought from the Government in 1921-3 after seeing war service. *Hecate* and *Dido* were scrapped in 1930 and 1931 and *Daphne* was sold to the Southern Railway in 1939 and scrapped at Eastleigh in April 1949. Stephens also brought in a trio of LNWR 0-6-0 coal engines.

The Shropshire & Montgomeryshire Light Railway opened amid local fanfare in Shrewsbury on April 13, 1911. The first passenger trains ran to Llanymynech with the branch to Criggion reopening to goods on February 21 and to passengers on July 27, 1912, with a mineral traffic interchange yard at Meole Brace. The Criggion branch attracted tourists in the form of walkers from the Shrewsbury area who used the trains to reach the nearby Breiddon Hills. There was a turntable in the field beyond Criggon station.

During the years that followed, the line to Criggion became a part of Britain's emerging tourist industry. Walkers from the Shrewsbury area used the line to travel to Criggion and then hike up the nearby Breiddon Hills. Huts were arranged around a turntable beyond the station with basic sleeping facilities for hikers.

Stephens also brought in a second-hand London County Council horse-drawn double-deck tramcar which was adapted to be used behind Gazelle by ripping out the top deck and stairs. The ripped-out upper deck seats saw a second life as platform seats at the line's stations.

Stephens' latest cut-price railway recorded modest returns for its first year.

LSWR 'Ilfracombe Goods' 0-6-0 *Pyramus* or *Thisbe* at Kinnerley on July 18, 1919. Of the three Class 282s bought for the railway, *Thisbe* lasted the longest, being withdrawn in 1941. CSRM

Former LNWR freight 0-6-0 collier with four-wheeled ex-Midland Railway passenger brake van No.1 and carriage at Kinnerley. CSRM

LSWR Class 282 'Ilfracombe Goods' 0-6-0 No. 5 *Pyramus* with three four-wheel-carriages. These were light engines constructed by Beyer Peacock & Co. between 1873 and 1880 to the order of W G Beattie for working the steeply graded Barnstaple-Ilfracombe line, which was then newly opened. Bought second-hand by Stephens, Nos. 0283, 0300 and 0324 became Shropshire & Montgomery Railway Nos. 6 *Thisbe*, 5 *Pyramus* and 3 *Hesperus*. CSRM

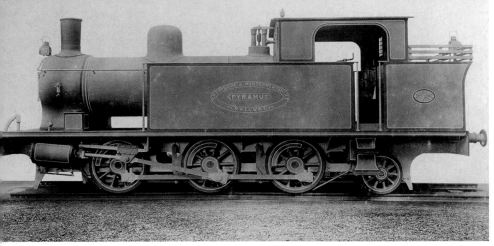

The original No. 5 *Pyramus*, one of a pair of Hawthorne Leslie 0-6-2Ts built in 1911 for the Shropshire & Montgomeryshire Light Railway, the other being No. 6 *Thisbe*. The only new locomotives bought for the line, both were sold to the government in 1916 and appear to have first gone to the Cannock Chase Military Railway. *Thisbe* went to the Woolmer Instructional Military Railway while *Pyramus* was sold for industrial use in 1921. Their Shropshire & Montgomeryshire Light Railway identities were given to two of the LSWR 'Ilfracombe Goods' 0-6-0s bought for the line. TYNE & WEAR ARCHIVES & MUSEUMS

proposal was to create three Central Ammunition Depots (CAD) in easily hewn and relatively horizontal rocks: one in the south (Monkton Farleigh); one in the north of England (Longtown, Cumbria); and one in the Midlands (Nesscliffe).

CAD Nesscliffe was developed by the War Office/Ministry of Defence after war broke out. To service the extensive property, the MoD leased the all-but defunct railway from June 1, 1941 and built extensive additional service tracks along the 8¾ miles of line from Maesbrook to the former Ford and Crossgate station.

Like a typical ammunition depot, the site was laid out over an extensive area to avoid total destruction should an accidental explosion occur, or the site be attacked by the Luftwaffe. The site

Former LNWR 0-6-0 freight 0-6-0 No.8236 in the platform, Shrewsbury Abbey Foregate on September 5, 1935. CSRM

Ilfracombe Goods 0-6-0 No. 5 *Pyramus* with three four-wheel-carriages. CSRM

However, the First World War brought about the start of an action replay of the losses incurred by the Potts Line. Furthermore, as with other Stephens light railways, competition from motor buses rendered passenger services unprofitable again.

Mineral traffic on the Criggion branch remained healthy but its passenger services ended in 1929 and *Gazelle* was taken out of use.

In a vain bid to bolster declining passenger services between Shrewsbury and Llanymynech, a two-car Ford railcar set was brought in by Stephens, but to no avail. Designed for use in city streets, the railcars proved deeply unpopular with passengers because of the noise made by the pressed steel wheels. Passenger services on the railway's main line were withdrawn on November 6, 1913.

However, the Criggion quarry traffic was boosted in the early Thirties with stone supplied for national building contracts. A trio of LNWR 0-6-0 'Coal Engines' were brought in to handle it.

The recession of the 1930s killed off this traffic and the line went back to running just a daily goods-only service, although occasional bank holiday excursions for tourists continued until 1937.

WARTIME AND AFTERWARDS

By September 1, 1939, with the declaration of war against Nazi Germany, the Shropshire & Montgomeryshire Light Railway was on its last legs traffic-wise. In May 1940 its directors looked to close it between Kinnerley and Meole Brace, leaving only the severed ends of the line for quarry traffic, plus the increasing petrol traffic at Abbey Foregate.

However, the war gave the railway a new lease of life. During the 1930s, there was a recognition of a need to provide secure storage for munitions within the United Kingdom. The

was made up of four sub-sites, Kinnerley, Pentre, Ford, and Argoed, each capable of storing around 55,000 tons of shells.

There was also a sub-site at Loton Park, under the Alberbury medieval deer park, used from 1943 for the storage of both incendiary ammunition and chemical weapons shells. It was one of two CW depots operated in co-operation with and guarded by the United States Army Air Forces, the second being in Shepton Mallet, Somerset. Locomotives and their drivers were provided by the Royal Engineers, which also maintained the extensive network. The main servicing depot for rolling

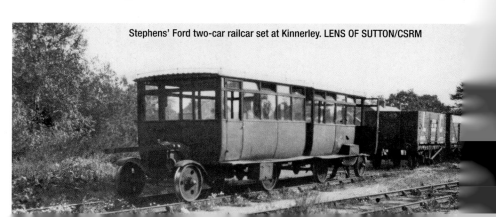

Stephens' Ford two-car railcar set at Kinnerley. LENS OF SUTTON/CSRM

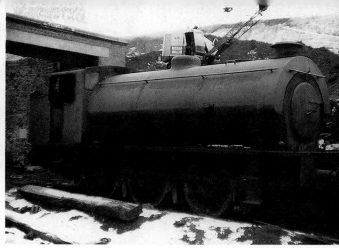

After withdrawal in 1950, when all of the line's locomotives and stock were taken over by the GWR, No. 1 *Gazelle* was saved and sent to the Transportation Centre of the Royal Engineers at Longmoor in Hampshire in 1950 where it was displayed on the edge of the parade ground. When the Longmoor Military Railway, an early preservation venue, closed in 1970, *Gazelle* was reclaimed by the Science Museum and displayed at York Railway Museum, before moving again to the Museum of Army Transport at Beverley. In 1997 *Gazelle* was relocated to Tenterden, as described in Chapter 18. BEN BROOKSBANK*

Robert Stephenson & Hawthorns Austerity 0-6-0ST No.7099 of 1943 served on the Shropshire & Montgomeryshire Railway as War Department No.75063 (later No.125). It was subsequently sold to the National Coal Board and ended up at Maerdy Colliery where it is pictured on New Year's Day, 1971, the year when it was scrapped on site. HUGH LLEWELLYN*

The Shrewsbury Railway Heritage Trust's recently-restored Abbey Foregate station building. SHREWSBURY RAILWAY HERITAGE TRUST

stock was on the stub-junction of the Criggion branch.

The 1941 locomotive fleet of *Gazelle*, *Hesperus* and the three LNWR 0-6-0s was supplemented by various War Department locomotives, including GWR 2301 class Dean goods 0-6-0s and Hunslet Austerity 0-6-0STs.

Two of the War Department locomotives were LNER J15 0-6-0s No. 7541 and 7835 (renumbered WD221 and WD212) which had been withdrawn by the LNER and sold to London Film Productions for the 1936 film Knight Without Armour starring Marlene Dietrich and Robert Donat. The two locomotives were moved to Denham film studios and modified to look more Russian as that was where the film was set.

The locomotives were then sold to the War Department and worked on the Shropshire & Montgomeryshire Railway. However, during their war service both were involved in incidents and returned to Stratford in 1944 where they were subsequently scrapped.

AFTER THE WAR

From 1945, the Criggion branch was operated by Sentinel DE class 100hp steam locomotive No. 7026 of 1928 which was owned by the British Quarrying Company.

The line was nationalised from January 1, 1948, and became part of British Railways. General goods services on the Criggion branch ended on May 2, 1949, after which the branch became a siding operated by the quarry shunting locomotive.

Ammunition storage on the site officially stopped in 1959, and the railway finally closed in 1960, as the loss of the British Empire reduced the need for military depots. The ammunition depot closed in 1961, and all the track had been lifted by 1962. The operational locomotives were moved to the Longmoor Military Railway, while

Foxfield Railway-based Beyer Peacock 0-4-0ST No. 1827 of 1878 brought steam to today's Tanat Valley Light Railway at Nantmawr in November 2009. The location was the furthest point reached by the Shropshire & Montgomeryshire Railway. OSRAIL*

Ruston & Hornsby 88DR 4w diesel mechanical shunter No. 338416 of 1953 *Crabtree* at the temporary wooden platform at Nantmawr on today's Tanat Valley Light Railway during the Heritage Open Days in September 2018. TK420*

the non-operational ones were sold off commercially.

Since 1961 the site has been part of the Nesscliffe Training Area, used constantly through the year by helicopters from the Defence Helicopter Flying School at RAF Shawbury for training pilots and crew.

The Abbey Foregate yard was latterly used as an oil dispatch yard, from 1960 after the line closed. British Railways Western Region added a spur onto the Severn Valley line at Burnt Mill so that oil tankers could be unloaded into road tankers on the site. This arrangement lasted until 1988 when the track was in too bad a state to continue.

In the late 1960s, the water column from Abbey Foregate was removed to the preserved Kent & East Sussex Railway, a home-from-home for a piece of the Stephens empire!

ABBEY FOREGATE TODAY

Abbey Foregate station has been restored and converted into a visitor centre which outlines the stories of the succession of railways which ran into it. Overseen by the Shrewsbury Railway Heritage Trust, the building restoration was started by Shrewsbury Town Council in 2009 and completed by Shropshire Council.

The visitor centre was opened for the public for the first time on the weekend of September 8/9, 2012. A base for guided railway/industrial heritage walks; talks, and art exhibitions, but primarily the

building will benefit the local community by providing a meeting place for a variety of local groups. The centre is managed by a group of voluntary board members and is registered as a charitable trust.

The Shrewsbury Railway Heritage Trust was established as a charity in July 2003 to advance the education of the public about the railway heritage of Shrewsbury and its region through lectures, publications and other means, while collecting relevant documents, conserving and interpreting material while maintaining a museum in which to display it.

Further details can be found at https://shrewsburyrailwayheritage.com or via email at srht1860@outlook.com

THE LAST OPERATION LENGTH

In 1998, a group of local railway enthusiasts explored the viability of preserving as much as possible of the former Tanat Valley Light Railway, which ran from Llynclys Junction in England to Llangynog in Wales, and which had connections with the Potts Line.

They set up a modern-day Tanat Valley Light Railway Company (TVLR) which in 2004 acquired a two-mile section of disused trackbed.

Based in its Nantmawr Visitor Centre at the former lime kilns in Nantmawr, at the terminus of the Potts Line, it operated its first trains over a third-of-a-mile of the track in November 2009, 46 years after the last steam engine saw service and providing the first ever steam passenger service over the length.

The TVLR won the Pride of Shropshire award in 2010 for the best environmental project in the county, for the woodland walk and footpath complex. The railway plans to eventually operate trains from Nantmawr to Llanddu by Blodwell Quarry. It has a Ruston & Hornsby 88 diesel shunter nicknamed *Crabtree*, five Class 107 DMU vehicles and a Class 309 EMU from the closed Coventry Electric Railway Museum at Baginton, which now serves as a museum and buffet train.

Around 2016 the railway obtained a portable industrial monorail, designed by Road Machines (Drayton) Ltd and used for construction projects in the mid-20th century. Since 2017, the centre has been the permanent home for the collection of the late Richard Morris, who owned the Gloddfa Ganol narrow gauge railway and mining centre at Blaenau Ffestiniog which closed in 1997. It comprises the largest collection of industrial monorail equipment in the UK including more than 70 engines and a large number of wagons, each of the engines carrying the name of the place where it originally operated.

However, its star exhibit in this field is undoubtedly an 0-2-0 built by Richard Morris himself, and which is believed to be the only true operating monorail steam engine in the world. What would Colonel Stephens have made of that?

RAILWAY RETREATS

www.railwayretreats.co.uk
Tel: 01797 253850
Email: bookings@railwayretreats.co.uk

First-Class
Self Catering Holiday
Accommodation

MK1 Plum & Custard

• Sleeps 6 • Two double bedrooms • Bunk bedroom • Family bathroom
• En-suite bathroom • Open plan lounge and dining area
• Full kitchen with everything you need
The carriage also offers you the best view of the station, surrounding
countryside and golden sunsets from the elevated glass balcony.

Guns & Roses Ammunition Wagon (Sleeps 2+2)

• Double bedroom • Sofa bed • Shower room/WC • Microwave • Fridge
• Barbecue • Individual garden • Fully insulated • Double glazed and
heated with great views of the station platform.

GWR TOAD Brake Van (Sleeps 2)

• Fitted kitchen/dining area • Double bedroom • Free Sat TV • En suite
shower room/WC • Fully insulated • Double glazed and heated
The fully glazed kitchen and balcony providing panoramic views of
the station platform and Rother Valley

All our carriages are situated on the beautiful Kent and East Sussex
border within Northiam Steam Railway Station, a working station.
You don't even need to leave the carriage to get the full railway
experience as the steam trains will pull up at the station just
20ft away!

Chapter 9

No. 1 *Clevedon* heads nears Wick St Lawrence with a train to Weston in June 1937. W VAUGHAN-JENKINS/
COLONEL STEPHENS MUSEUM

THE WESTON, CLEVEDON & PORTISHEAD RAILWAY

A railway built to link three neighbouring coastal towns in principle should have been a success story. Not so the Weston, Clevedon & Portishead Railway, which floundered financially almost from the start and closed after the Second World War started, despite much input from Colonel Stephens and his successor William Austen.

The Weston, Clevedon & Portishead Railway (WCPR) was the only form of communication – road, railway or footpath – to directly link the three North Somerset coastal towns in its name.

Weston-super-Mare was still a small village until the 19th century when it became a seaside resort, with parks and terraces similar to the more grandiose Regency Bath; two piers were built. When Isambard Kingdom Brunel built the Bristol & Exeter Railway, at first it bypassed smaller towns on the way. However, when the main line opened in 1841, a horse-drawn single-track branch line opened to Weston, converting to steam seven years later. In 1866, a loop from the main line was authorised, with a new station built in 1881.

Partly owing to the large tidal range in the Bristol Channel, the second highest in the world after Newfoundland's Bay of Fundy, the low tide mark in Weston Bay is a mile from the seafront. Although the beach itself is sandy, low tide uncovers areas of thick mud, hence the nickname, Weston-super-Mud, and the sea has a distinctive brown hue, caused by sediment washed down the river from as far away as the Welsh hills. To the north of the town is Sand Bay and Sand Point which marks the lower limit of the Severn Estuary and the start of the Bristol Channel.

Beyond Sand Point, the River Yeo firmly divides the flatlands around Weston from those to the north.

On another hill which rises above the fen-like wetlands is Clevedon, which grew in the Victorian period as a seaside resort and in the 20th century as a dormitory town. It too has a seaside pier, and retains much of its 19th century charm, being used for location filming for TV series such as Broadchurch and the 2019 version of Jane Austen's unfinished 1817 novel Sanditon. A branch line from a junction at Yatton was opened to Clevedon in 1847, also as part of the Bristol & Exeter Railway, and was similarly laid to 7ft 0¼in broad gauge.

A fairly short hop by road from Clevedon is Portishead, which has a long history as a fishing port. As a royal manor it expanded rapidly during the early 19th century around the docks,

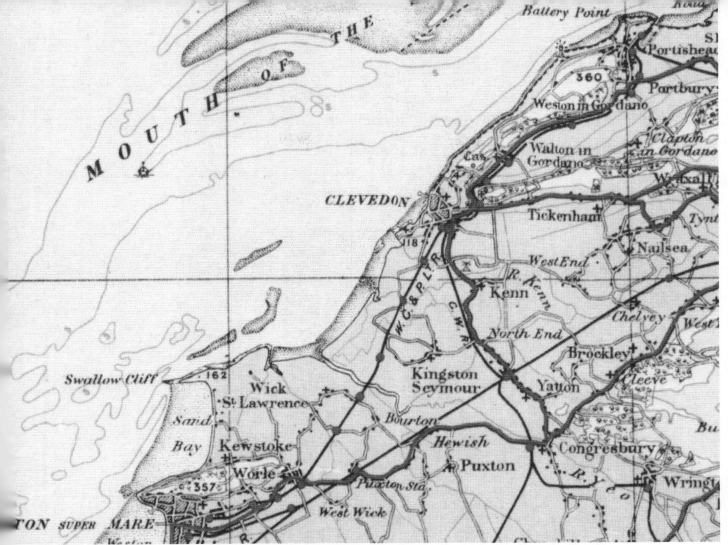

Edwardian four inches to the mile map showing the Weston, Portishead and Clevedon Railway and the other lines serving those towns.

with supporting transport infrastructure. In 1867 the Bristol & Portishead Pier & Railway opened a broad gauge branch line from Bedminster to Portishead, operated by the Bristol & Exeter Railway, and which became part of the GWR in 1884.

However, because of the local terrain, it was awkward to travel between the three towns, and indeed still is, without taking a circuitous route by road.

In December 1884, the Weston-super-Mare, Clevedon & Portishead (Steam) Tramways Company drew up a scheme to lay a standard gauge tram line to link the towns. Its prime mover was Mr JFR Daniel, secretary to the Bristol & Portishead Railway, who later became managing director of the WCPR.

An Act of Parliament empowering the construction of the tramway was passed in Aug 1885, but due to various legal and financial problems, the time limit of this legislation ran out and further Acts were needed in July 1890 and Dec 1891.

The line was to run on the street along the Boulevard in Weston and from then off-road apart from level crossings. The construction of the Weston to Clevedon section started in 1887.

However, the project suffered financial delays, which persisted to the point where the sleepers rotted and needed

to be replaced. Also, the track along the Boulevard was lifted before the tramway opened due to complaints from Weston-super-Mare Urban District Council about the rails protruding above the level of the road surface.

The tramway between Weston and Clevedon opened on December 1, 1897, the journey taking a little over an hour. On Boxing Day that year, 1254 passengers were carried.

The first coaches supplied to the line were built in mahogany with wrought ironwork and gates at each end by the Lancaster Railway Carriage & Wagon Company and had originally been destined for the Argentine Republic Railway, and were of typical American and decidedly non-British appearance.

Two years after the opening, the tramway was designated a light railway and the name was changed to the Weston,

Weston-super-Mare's Ashcombe Road terminus on August 1, 1927, 13.8 miles from Portishead. The Weston Clevedon & Portishead Railway Group asked Weston-super-Mare council to erect an information board on the site of the station and name the lane which now covers the trackbed Colonel Stephens Way. The path was duly named and MP John Penrose unveiled the information board on December 9, 2011. PETER STRANGE/ COLONEL STEPHENS MUSEUM

An Edwardian hand-coloured postcard of Anchor Head, one of Weston-super-Mare's seafront beauty sports. ROBIN JONES COLLECTION

An early 20th century hand-coloured view of the Portishead terminus. The extension to here from Clevedon opened on August 7, 1907, but it caused severe financial problems which led to the railway company entering receivership in November 1909, and it never recovered.

Portishead never took off as a seaside resort in its own right and nowadays is a commuter settlement for Bristol. However, in summer 1905, its shingly foreshore proved popular. ROBIN JONES COLLECTION

Clevedon & Portishead Light Railway Company.

Portishead was linked to Clevedon by horse-drawn omnibus, and residents of the latter town were wary about a railway running through its streets once an extension to its northern neighbour was built. The compromise was to have a flagman leading the trains along the streets at 4mph.

The Act of Parliament authorising the extension to Portishead was passed in August 1899, and despite the company floundering into yet more financial difficulties through poor management, it finally opened on August 7, 1907. However, in November 1909, the company went into receivership – and never recovered from it. Indeed, the WCPR spent 31 of its 43 years in the hands of receivers.

IN COMES THE COLONEL

The company tried to force the hand of the GWR into making a takeover bid, by threatening to link the WCPR with the Somerset & Dorset Joint Railway, which ran to Burnham-on-Sea, the next resort to the south. However, creditors rallied round Cuthbert E Heath, considered the driving force behind the company, and a man with a track record of saving light railways was brought in: Holman F Stephens.

He drew up several plans to boost the railway's appeal, including a coal-field branch, which never happened, and a short branch to a wharf at Wick St Lawrence on the River Yeo, which did, in 1915.

However, like similar light railways throughout Britain, the WCPR was being hit hard by competition from road traffic, and while under Stephens it could at last pay its day-to-day operating costs, the historic debt could not be lessened.

Among the innovations introduced by Stephens were railmotors, in the form of a small Drewry internal combustion-powered railway and trailer, and a larger Drewry vehicle which had been built for the Southern Railway, plus a petrol shunter for the wharf. He also bought small coasters to carry goods to and from the wharf, but these were not successful.

Following Stephens' death in 1931, Austen took over as manager until the railway closed. In 1939, the Railway Executive Committee met to decide which light railways should be taken over if war with Nazi Germany broke out. After some debate regarding the merits of the fact that the WCPR served road-stone quarries, the Ministry of Transport decided against taking over the WCPR in the event of an emergency, and when the Government took control of the nation's railway on September 1, 1939, it was excluded.

Due to an ever-worsening financial state, the company applied for a court order to close the line. The historically-hostile GWR bought the line (but not the land) to use it for storage, and up to 200 coal wagons were initially stored on the line. It was decided to lift the track for use in the war effort, and it was cleared between October 1942 and late 1943. However, the legality of the ownership of the land was a long-running issue that was never properly resolved. The WCPR land still belonged to the company though it no longer existed.

From the outset, the WCPR had used a motley collection of second-hand locomotives and rolling stock as the mainstay of its services. In 1925, Stephens acquired 1877-built London, Brighton & South Coast Railway 'Terrier' 0-6-0T No. 43 Gipsyhill, later No. 643, and renumbered and renamed No.2 Portishead. In 1937, Austen brought in a second 'Terrier', 1875-built No. 53 Ashtead, later No. 653/ Southern Railway No. 2653.

When the WCR passed into the hands of the GWR in 1940, the Swindon empire inherited both 'Terriers', a classic feature of the fleet of its arch rivals the Southern, and totally out of place on GWR branch lines. AS GWR No.6, Ashtead was withdrawn in January 1948, and Portishead, as GWR No. 5, lasted in British Railways service until 1954.

None of the other WCPR locomotives survived.

AN EARLY HERITAGE LINE?

In 1951, a group of volunteers led by transport historian LTC Rolt saved the Talyllyn Railway in central Wales by running it themselves, and in doing so kick-started the heritage railway movement.

Their exploits inspired the classic 1953 Ealing comedy, The Titfield Thunderbolt,

Sharp Stewart 2-4-0T *Hesperus* was built in 1876 for the Watlington & Princes Risborough Railway, and became GWR No. 1384. It is seen still carrying its GWR at Portishead in 1911. It was scrapped in 1937. COLONEL STEPHENS MUSEUM

Bathing machines to the fore on Clevedon's main beach at high tide in 1905. The agricultural village of Clevedon took off as a seaside resort in Victorian times after the Bristol & Exeter Railway opened a broad gauge branch from Yatton on the main line on July 28, 1847. Technically, Clevedon lies on the Severn estuary, as the sea is considered to start at Sand Point just north of Weston-super-Mare, although it lies on the second biggest tidal range in the world outside the Bay of Fundy in Newfoundland and has a foreshore comprising of sand, shingle and mud. ROBIN JONES COLLECTION

Dübs 2-4-0T No.1 Clevedon at Clevedon Gas Works in September, 1937. It was scrapped at Swindon in 1940. PETER STRANGE/COLONEL STEPHENS MUSEUM

starring Stanley Holloway, Naunton Wayne, George Relph and John Gregson, about a group of enthusiasts trying to keep their branch line open after British Railways decided to close it.

Around that time, there was an attempt by Bristol enthusiasts Mr S Jones-Frank and Major W D I Gunn to reopen part of the WCPR as a 2ft 8in gauge railway for tourists.

In March 1955, the British Transport Commission duly approved the foundation of the North Somerset Light Railway Company, the first private railway company to be floated since nationalisation.

The company planned to run 12 trains a day on a 6½-mile section of the route between Clevedon and the outskirts of Weston at Worle.

A slight deviation from the original trackbed would be built from just before

No. 5 with mixed train from Portishead near Clevedon Saw Mills in September 1937. COLONEL STEPHENS MUSEUM

The loading of milk churns at Worle on July 31, 1927, following an accident a day earlier. COLONEL STEPHENS MUSEUM

Manning Wardle 0-6-0ST No. 5 and train arriving at Clevedon on May 17, 1937. PETER STRANGE/COLONEL STEPHENS MUSEUM

Had those ambitious plans succeeded, I have no doubt that a rebuilt railway would have established itself as a significant tourist attraction, firstly in an age when most Britons still took summer holiday in their own country. Compared to the original, it would have run only when season demand dictated. Had it been running today, it would have made a sizeable input to the local tourist economy. Holman Fred Stephens would definitely have approved.

In November 2006, the Weston, Clevedon & Portishead Railway Group was formed to preserve what is left of the line, and to promote its heritage to the public.

THREE TOWNS LINKED AGAIN
In late 2018, it was announced that a 39-year dream to turn part of the trackbed into a cyclepath and walkway would be realised at long last.

A replica of the former Wick St Lawrence Halt is set to be built as part of North Somerset Council's £2,450,000 scheme to establish a 'pier to pier' cycle

A barge discharging coal at Wick St Lawrence wharf in 1921. The boat may have been owned by the railway. EDWIN HAZELL/ COLONEL STEPHENS MUSEUM

the original Clevedon station to a new terminus in Salthouse Fields.

The next year, the company bought Peckett 0-4-02ST No. 1808 *Septimus* of 1930 which had been built for the Furzebrook Tramway in the Isle of Purbeck.

Very sadly, the plans for the 'new' railway never bore fruit. *Septimus* was returned to its Bristol maker and was scrapped there in 1962.

No. 1 *Clevedon* heads nears Wick St Lawrence with a train to Weston in June 1937.
W VAUGHAN-JENKINS/COLONEL STEPHENS MUSEUM

route between Weston and Clevedon, it was announced.

The 0.9-mile shared path for use by walkers, cyclists and horse riders will for part of the way use an existing farm track built on the route of the WCPR from Wick Lane in Wick St Lawrence to Yeo Bank Lane at Kingston Seymour. The project will also involve a new agricultural crossing over the River Yeo to keep farm animals separate from path users, plus additional highway works in Kewstoke and Clevedon and road markings.

Planning permission for the scheme was granted in December 2018. The council was awarded £645,000 by the Rural Payments Agency to cover the

Large Drewry railcar and trailer at Clevedon on June 25, 1938. HC CASSERLEY/ COLONEL STEPHENS MUSEUM

'Terrier' 0-6-0T No. 4 with ex-Taff Vale Railway coach and two wagons ~ching Walton Park, bound for Portishead, in December 1937. PETER ~E/COLONEL STEPHENS MUSEUM

Known on the LBSCR as 'Terrier' No. 53 *Ashtead*, WCPR No. 4 was inherited by the GWR in 1940 and became that company's No. 6. It was withdrawn eight years later. COLONEL STEPHENS MUSEUM

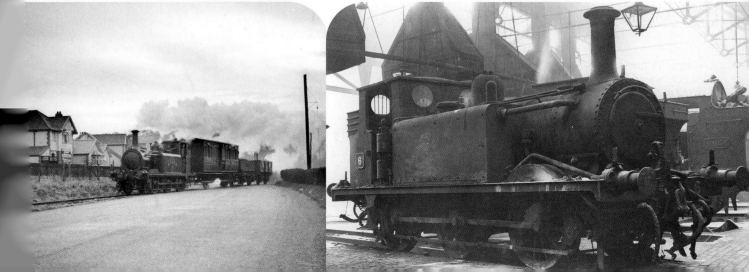

Were the crowds waving to the last train on May 18, 1940? COLONEL STEPHENS MUSEUM

construction costs of the path, and in May 2020, Highways England granted £1.3 million towards the project, which will reduce the distance to travel between the towns from 17 miles using main roads to 13 miles on minor roads and off-road paths and creating the first direct link between Weston and Clevedon since the railway closed on May 18, 1940.

Remote Wick St Lawrence Halt lay at the halfway point between Weston and Clevedon nearly a mile from the village, but nonetheless was manned until 1938. It had a passing loop, a wooden waiting room and ticket office. The replica halt is earmarked for the entrance to the cycleway off Wick Road.

The new cycleway – which was proposed as long ago as 1979 with a group set up to campaign for the project now having more than 1300 supporters – will be promoted as a recreational route from Weston's Grand Pier to Clevedon Pier. The project forms the central section of the council's proposed 'Coastal Towns Cycle Route', linking Bristol,

Portishead, Clevedon, Weston and Brean.

THE PHOENIX COACH
One item of rolling stock from the WCPR has not only survived but has been returned to pristine condition for high-profile use – on London Underground!

In 1892, the Sheffield coachbuilding firm of Cravens built four-wheeled first class carriage No. 353 for the Metropolitan Railway. It was one of a type known as Jubilee carriages, because the first examples were constructed in 1887, the year of Queen Victoria's Golden Jubilee.

As the Metropolitan Railway empire grew, the Jubilee coaches were rendered obsolete, too small to cope with the volume of traffic, and so in 1907, No. 353 was sold to the WCPR, where it became the line's No. 12.

After the WCPR closed, the GWR sold No. 12 for use by military tailors at Shrivenham in Oxfordshire. The coach later became a US army mess room and

after the war it became used as a private dwelling and antiques shop and later became a farm building.

In 1974, the coach was offered to London Transport Museum in part exchange for a platform seat. The museum kept it in unrestored condition, firstly at Syon Park and latterly at its Acton depot store. In 2011, with celebrations to mark the 150th anniversary of the Metropolitan Railway at the planning stage, the Heritage Lottery Fund agreed to finance the biggest share of a £572,000 restoration package for the coach. The Friends of London Transport Museum group provided the rest of the cash.

As well as the restoration of the coach itself, the project included an important skills transfer element, enabling apprentices to learn the skill of coach restoration and to transfer that practical knowledge to other restoration projects.

In August that year, the coach body – its chassis having long since been scrapped – was taken to the Ffestiniog

The colours of the rainbow sharply contrast with the silt-laden brown waters of the Bristol Channel around Clevedon Pier, a railway relic 'by the back door'. While working on the Midland Railway main line, civil engineer William Henry Barlow, the designer of St Pancras station, patented his own design of rail in 1849 to overcome the problem of rotten sleepers. Barlow rail, as it became known, was widely used on the GWR and associated lines. In 1866, it was decided to build a pier at Clevedon so that pleasure steamers could call. Its engineers, John Grover and Richard Ward, bought 37 tons of redundant Barlow rails which had been supplied to Brunel's South Wales Railway and used them to build the pier. The rails were bolted together to form the legs of the elegant 1024ft eight-span pier which had to withstand the powerful currents of the Bristol Channel and its immense tidal range. Described by the late Poet Laureate Sir John Betjeman as "the most beautiful pier in England," the pier was officially opened on March 29, 1869 and given Grade I listed building protection in 2001. ROBIN JONES

Welsh Highland Railways' Boston Lodge Works.

Over 15 months, the coach was rebuilt to original condition inside and out, and in mid-November 2012, was taken back outside the historic works and mounted on the modified chassis of Southern Railway parcels van No. 847. Craftsmen had worked round the clock to get it ready in time for et 150.

The gleaming carriage, finished with old leaf and carrying 12 coats of varnish on the exterior and nine on the inside woodwork, bore little resemance to the sorry-looking hulk which d arrived at Porthmadog. However, % of the wooden frame is the original aterial.

The carriage was originally fitted with s lighting, forbidden under present y safety regulations. Modern LED

Wick St Lawrence Halt in 1938. It is now set to be rebuilt as a gateway to a long-awaited cyclepath which will make use of the original trackbed. PETER STRANGE

The only railway flag in Clevedon today is flown by the excellent 15in gauge Clevedon Miniature Railway in Salthouse Fields, where the line's green 'Black Five' 4-6-0 No. 5305 is seen in action in May 2014. ROBIN JONES

The remains of the railway wharf at Wick St Lawrence, which was served by a short goods branch north of the Weston, Clevedon & Portishead Railway halt. JOHN THO
CREATIVE COMMONS

Weston, Clevedon & Portishead Railway coach No.12 ended up in use on a farm in Shrivenham, Oxfordshire. **LONDON TRANSPORT MUSEUM**

PMV underframe, it was necessary to bed in the suspension and brakes, and to build confidence in the performance and dynamic behaviour of the vehicle.

Once safe operation at 25mph had been demonstrated, the carriage was tested to 40mph, then to a maximum higher speed of 50mph the following day. The railway had been granted derogation by the Office of Rail Regulation (since renamed the Office of Rail and Road) for undertaking the high speed test.

The Institute of Railway Research carried out the safety assurance work for the carriage and conducted the instrumentation and testing of the vehicle with support from London Underground and Ffestiniog Railway representatives.

From there, it was a case of back to London, in readiness for the test runs and the big day.

No. 353 – in which Colonel Stephens had likely travelled on the WCPR – played a starring role in the Met 150 celebrations, its restored magnificence often threatening to steal the show.

London Transport Museum's beautifully-restored Metropolitan Railway coach No. 353 which ran on the Weston, Clevedon & Portishead Railway for more than three decades. ROBIN JONES

lamps have instead given the appearance of gas mantles to maintain authenticity. In November 2012, it was loaded onto a lorry for onward transport to the Great Central Railway at Loughborough, the world's only double-track heritage trunk line. There, No. 353 underwent test runs.

As the carriage had not previously run in its current form using a modified

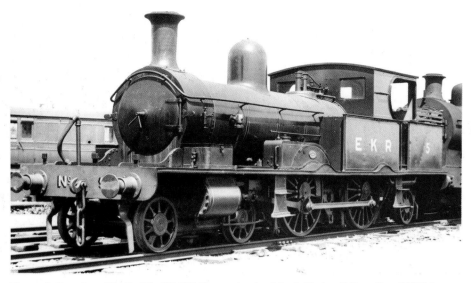

4-CEP No. 7105 at Shepherdswell during the East Kent Railway EMU gala on September 15, 2019. JUSTIN & TERRY FOULGER RAILWAY PHOTOGRAPHY*

The greatest survivor of the East Kent Light Railways – London & South Western Railway Class 0415 Adams radial 4-4-2T No.5 – is seen at Shepherdswell on July 18, 1936. Built by Neilson & Company in 1885, it became LSWR No. 488, and was sold to the Ministry of Munitions in September 1917 for use at Ridham Salvage Depot in Sittingbourne. The EKLR bought it in April 1919, and sold it to the Southern Railway in March 1946. Used on the Lyme Regis branch as British Railways No. 30583, in was withdrawn in July 1961 and sold to the Bluebell Railway, where it is stored today. CSRM

THE EAST KENT LIGHT RAILWAYS

Colonel Stephens' portfolio of railways has often been described as his empire. However, the East Kent Light Railways (EKLR) included more than 40 separate statutory railways constructed, or planned but never built, to serve the East Kent coalfield. It may therefore be considered an empire within an empire, but it was not a very successful one at that.

It was railways that led to the discovery of coal seams beneath East Kent. On February 15, 1890, Francis Brady, chief engineer of the South Eastern Railway, conducted boring investigations for an early channel tunnel project at Shakespeare Cliff near Dover and made the initial find.

Shakespeare Colliery was duly established by speculator Arthur Burr in 1896 – but during 22 years of operations it never produced any commercial coal. Between 1896 and 1919, 38 boreholes were sunk to locate more coal in Kent. Exploration was carried out at Rushbourne, Hoads Wood in Sturry, Herne Bay, Reculver, Chitty and Chislet Park. Burr was convinced that Kent coal would make both himself and his investors rich.

However, the only worthwhile deposits were found 1500ft below the surface, making extraction difficult and costly. Burr had not realised the seams were so far down, nor that the seams were thin and folded and that the coal itself was of extremely poor quality.

Cosmetically-restored Avonside 0-6-0ST No. 2004 of 1927 *St Dunstan* at Shepherdswell on the East Kent Railway. *St Dunstan* worked at Snowdown Colliery, the deepest pit in the Kent coalfield. TRAIN PHOTOS

He hadn't taken the possibility of flooding into account either. An accident at Shakespeare Colliery on March 6, 1897, claimed the lives of eight men when there was a sudden inrush of water at a depth of 366ft.

Between 1904 and 1910, Burr established five more collieries, often finance by French investors, but none of them managed to produce coal for commercial sale until 1912. Indeed, Burr was always short of capital and forever sailing close to insolvency.

By 1910, he was manager or director of 22 different companies, all of which had his Kent Coal Concessions Ltd as a major shareholder.

Nonetheless, Burr was given the Freedom of Dover for being "one of the greatest benefactors Dover had ever known" and at the dinner, Sherlock Holmes creator Sir Arthur Conan Doyle, as guest speaker, predicted that coal would soon make the port into one of the six biggest cities in Britain.

Investors eventually began to realise than any profits generated by the Kent coalfield would be tiny when split between all the shares that had been issued, and Burr was accused of being a conman.

In 1914 he was forced to resign from all his posts and faced several legal actions for fraud and misuse of funds. Burr had judgements of £80,000 made against him and was declared bankrupt, with a judge declaring that he was "dangerous rogue". He died in 1919 with many legal actions against him still outstanding.

However, extensive plans had by 1914 been drawn up for a major exploitation of the coalfield which expanded rapidly in the late 1920s and early 1930s, with its maximum output reached in 1936.

A PLACE FOR RAILWAYS

In 1910, Burr's Kent Coal Concessions Ltd promoted the EKLR, which also contracted the firm to build the line. The line was originally titled the East Kent

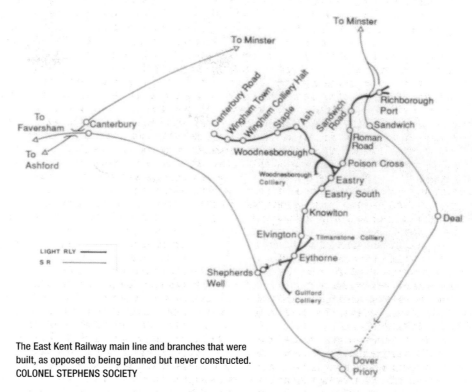

The East Kent Railway main line and branches that were built, as opposed to being planned but never constructed.
COLONEL STEPHENS SOCIETY

A large gang laying track during the construction of the railway. CSRM

EKLR No. 8 was a South Eastern & Chatham Railway O class 0-6-0 built in September 1891 by Sharp, Stewart and Company. Bought from the Southern Railway as No. A376 in 1928 and numbered 8, it was withdrawn March 1935 and cannibalised for spares. It is pictured at Wingham Canterbury Road in July 1932 or August 1933. CSRM

Mineral (Light) Railways when first proposed the year before. Burr conceived it as a system of lines directly linking at least nine collieries to a planned new coal port at Richborough, which had been known as Sandwich Haven before 1911.

It was also promoted by Christopher Solley of Sandwich Haven Wharves Syndicate at Sandwich, who dreamed of his town becoming a great port again. The site had a gravel pit and a quay on the Long Reach of the River Stour. The quay had been used during the construction of the Admiralty Harbour at Dover by contractor S Pearson & Sons, then one of the world's largest construction companies. This firm built a tramway,

Hudswell Clarke 0-6-0ST No.2 *Walton Park* in Shepherdswell platform with a mixed train, in June 1934. A Stephens empire seasoned veteran, the 1908-built locomotive was supplied new to the Weston, Clevedon & Portishead Light Railway and worked on the Shropshire & Montgomeryshire Light Railway before being transferred to the EKLR in 1913. Four years later, it was loaned to the Plymouth, Devonport & South Western Junction Railway. It ended its days at Hastings Gas Works and was scrapped in 1957. CSRM

EKLR 0-6-0T No.4 hauling open trucks. Built in 1917 by Kerr Stuart for the Inland Waterways Docks Department of the Royal Engineers, it was bought by the EKLR in 1917. It was scrapped by British Railways in 1949. CSRM

nicknamed Pearson's Railway, from a junction with the South Eastern & Chatham Railway at Richborough Castle to the gravel pit and quay.

Burr and fellow coalfield promoters may have chosen this site for their coal port rather than the more obvious Dover to the south. Before the First World War, Dover was intended to be the harbour of refuge for the Royal Navy's Channel Fleet, thereby leaving not much space for coal ships. However, by 1905 the Germans had steel cannon which could fire across the English Channel and hit Dover – rendering the port useless as a naval base, and in turn rendering the port at Richborough as a somewhat pointless venture in commercial terms.

The EKLR was authorised in 1911 to construct the coal wharf at Sandwich Haven. It was to have been built by St Augustine's Links Ltd, which had planned

to set out a golf course but then added a coal port and also established a subsidiary, Ebbsfleet Coal Syndicate, to build a coal mine. Again, the coal seams were found by a borehole dug in 1911 to be too thin, and the outbreak of the First World

War placed the coal port project on hold, although the golf course was built and is still there.

Holman F Stephens was engaged to plan the EKLR, and spent a huge amount of time surveying routes both for its main line and branches and obtaining the necessary Light Railway Orders, for which he ended up being either underpaid or not paid at all.

While the main thrust of the EKLR was to have been its main line to Richborough, the shortage of finance and difficulties of construction, combined with the need to bring in materials to build collieries at Tilmanstone and Guilford, led to the first length of the railway from Shepherdswell on the London & Chatham Railway's main line to Dover. Because of the poor state of the local roads of the day, a temporary line was brought into use by the autumn of 1911.

The railway slowly opened in stages from Shepherdswell to Richborough, and from Eastry to Wingham, which became renamed Wingham Colliery.

A double-track tunnel was bored at Golgotha near Eythorne. Stephens did not remove all the material from the double bore as a 'temporary' economy, and the line remained single track.

The tunnel was completed in October 1913, the same year that work ground to a halt because of a financial crisis, leaving only the lines to the collieries in full use.

Burr's collapsing portfolio of companies and the resulting financial scandal, combined with the outbreak of war, stopped further work on building the line in 1914. The EKLR took over direct control of its building from the Burr companies two years later. By then, Stephens had become both engineer and managing director.

His efforts led to both freight and passenger services from Shepherdswell to Wingham beginning on October 16, 1916. The original scheme had involved a line to Canterbury goods yard via Ickham, but authorisation was granted to build the line only as far as the Wingham parish

Wingham Canterbury Road station on July 29, 1939. The minimalist station was typical of many of those on the EKLR and indeed throughout the Colonel Stephens portfolio, being built as cheaply as possible. CSRM

boundary. Canterbury City Council had opposed the idea of a level crossing over the A28 at Sturry Road, and this proved a major stumbling block to the line's progress.

The Wingham line was extended unofficially by half a mile to Wingham Town in 1920, with a short spur running south to Wingham Engineering Ltd's works. However, by 1922, the mine works at Wingham and Guilford had both been abandoned together with the freight lines that had been built to serve them. A further extension to Wingham Canterbury Road opened in 1925. On April 18 that year, a passenger service, initially Saturdays only, from Eastry to Sandwich Road was launched, but it lasted only until October 31, 1928.

The EKLR had Stephens' stamp all over it: very basic platforms, minimalist facilities and a fleet of second-hand locomotives and rolling stock. Yet it was only because of his application of a very tight budget that the railway was able to open at all.

It settled down to running coal trains for Tilmanstone Colliery as its only profitable activity.

RICHBOROUGH PORT
The War Office took the port site at Richborough to build a massive transhipment camp in 1916. The Royal Engineers abandoned Pierson's Railway and built a new line from the SECR at Weatherlees Junction. An anonymous army official coined the name Richborough Port.

After hostilities ended, the SECR took over the port as temporary managers in 1919. Six years later, the facility was sold to Pearson & Dorman Long, the successor to the founding company.

The EKLR had been forced to place the completion of its main line to Richborough Port low down on its list of priorities, because the area was sealed off by the military during the war. It finally arrived at the port some time between 1920, when the War Office agreed to allow it to build junctions, and 1922. The official opening of the line between Eastry and Richborough Port has been given as 1925, but the first official goods traffic to the port did not arrive until 1929.

Pierson & Dorman Long sought to build a steelworks at the port, with new towns to house the workers at Woodnesborough and Ash and using coal from its Betteshanger Colliery. The company regarded the EKLR as an irritation, and did nothing to encourage it. Nonetheless, the EKLR did ship coal to Richborough for export from Snowdown Colliery from 1929 to the mid-Thirties, and brought in pit props for Tilmanstone Collierty by sea.

However, the Depression killed off the grandiose plans for Richborough Port. A main line link for coal traffic to Dover Eastern Harbour, via a tunnel under the castle, was authorised 1933. That came

South Eastern & Chatham Railway O class No. 372 was bought by Colonel Stephens from the Southern Railway in 1923 and it became the EKLR's No. 6. It was rebuilt to Class O1 specification in 1932. It is seen with a mixed train at Wingham on April 25, 1947. Withdrawn by British Railways on February 12, 1949, it was scrapped a fortnight later. CSRM

at the time when it was finally realised that the Kent coalfield was a commercial failure.

Richborough Port's railway network was abandoned before it was taken over by the National Coal Board in 1948. Silted up and long since derelict, Richborough is now one of Britain's 'lost' ports.

ULTIMATE FAILURE
Eventually, the Tilmanstone Colliery company objected to its rates and opened an aerial ropeway in competition with the railway, to the eastern arm of Dover Eastern Harbour in 1930. It too proved a failure, as the coal did not sell on the export market and mostly found a market in London. The ropeway continued to be used up to the outbreak of the Second World War, when it became too dangerous to use the harbour because of its exposed location. It was left in position until in 1952.

Stephens died in 1931 and, as elsewhere, was succeeded as EKLR general manager by his long-time assistant William Austen, who held the post until nationalisation in 1948. Under Austen, the dilapidated engine shed was rebuilt in 1938. The Second World War saw three rail-mounted guns operating on the line to Staple during 1940-2.

Loading wagons at Tilmanstone Colliery. CSRM

Rot, decay and inevitable disinterest saw the final passenger service of two trains each way on weekdays (down from three) run on October 30, 1948 following the nationalisation of British Railways which took control of the EKLR on May 3 that year. The passenger trains had run all but empty since colliery workers' trains had been withdrawn in 1930.

The line's once-sizeable agricultural traffic had by then been lost to road transport. Freight services from Eastry to Port Richborough officially ended on October 27, 1949, although no train had run along this length for several years and track was missing from the river bridge. The Richborough branch was officially

Two of the British Coal Snowdown Colliery locomotives in 1968.

Privately-owned Peckett 0-4-0ST No. 2087 of 1948 was the sole operational steam locomotive on the East Kent Railway. Originally named *Dafydd*, it was built as one of a batch of four for Courtaulds' Aber works at Flint. It was later transferred to Wolverhampton and then Red Scar plant, Preston, where it worked until replaced in 1968 by a diesel, having been rebuilt with parts from scrapped sister engine No. 2086 and renamed *Achilles*. EKR

closed on January 1, 1950, yet traffic over it appears to have carried on until the Wingham to Eastry section closed on July 25, 1950. The Eastry to Eythorne section closed on February 28, 1951.

However, the success of Tilmanstone Colliery allowed the EKLR main line to continue shipping its coal until it closed on March 1, 1984 during the miner's strike of 1984-85. The mine reopened briefly, but ceased production permanently in October 1986. After that this last section of the EKLR was officially closed.

The EKLR's trademark was failure; the collapse of the Burr empire, the intervention of the First World War, the failure of Richborough Port and the rivalry between the four successful East Kent mines ensured that the railway was never used to anything like its full capacity. One of these four mines, Bettesanger, even built its own railway rather than use the adjacent EKLR, while Snowdon and Chisley collieries were served by the national network.

Today, the majority of the EKLR has been reclaimed by Mother Nature, and only a few isolated landscape features can be made out from among the ploughed fields and thorny shrubs.

LAST LINE STANDING

The East Kent Railway Society was formed in November 1985, with the intention of saving and reopening the remaining 2¼ miles of line. Its volunteers had to wait until 1989 before they could clear the vast amounts of vegetation that had taken over the railway since closure.

The heritage-era East Kent Railway has transformed the station area and its surroundings at Shepherdswell, with a

replica of the original station building and platform being built, along with new access roads, car parks, toilet blocks, a café and picnic areas.

In 1993, a Light Railway Order was granted, permitting regular passenger trains to run again on the East Kent Railway after an absence of more than four decades. The heritage line ran its first train in 1995.

A new platform was constructed on the site of Eythorne station and the former signalbox from Selling was moved to the northern end of the platform in the mid-1990s.

The railway also owns the Barham signalbox from the closed Elham Valley Line. Now at Shepherdswell, it houses a detailed mural painting of the old East Kent Railway route.

The revived line also owns The Knees, an extensive ancient woodland, which is used as an educational resource and for woodland walks; the springtime bluebells are a popular attraction.

The railway hosts other heritage organisations including the Southern Electric Group, EKR Trolleybus Group and the 427 Locomotive Group and recently the Network SouthEast Railway Society. Today the East Kent Railway is a preservation haven for redundant Southern Region electric stock unwanted by other heritage lines but richly deserving to be saved. Such stock has to be locomotive hauled as no heritage line has

the necessary third-rail pick-up to run them using their own power.

If we are serious about railway preservation, we should save for posterity a cross-section of the system, not just the 'popular bits' such as steam locomotives. In this respect, the modestly proportioned modern-day East Kent Railway is providing a splendid service to the nation's transport heritage.

In 2020, the East Kent Railway took delivery of two items of traction which would undeniably have enthused Colonel Stephens, in the form of two Class 142 Pacer DMU sets following their mass withdrawal from main line service.

Built by British Rail Engineering Limited at its Litchurch Lane Works in Derby between 1985 and 1987, their bodies are based on that of the original Leyland National bus; indeed, many fixtures and fittings of the bus can be found on the units.

Following decades of complaints from passengers about the rough riding and lack of comfort of the Pacers, the Government ordered them to be removed from main line service by 2020.

On the other hand, the Pacers have been praised for saving services on some rural lines which might otherwise have been withdrawn if only more expensive rolling stock had been available. Pacers have also proved economical to operate, achieving 10 miles to the gallon, and both units will be used on running days when passenger numbers are low. Numerous other heritage lines have also seized the chance to take redundant Pacers on board.

While the type has long been associated with the north of England, and not Kent, the arrival of the pair is another string to the bow of the East Kent Railway, and conjures up visions of the Ford railcars that the colonel introduced on several of his lines at a time when road transport was in its ascendancy.

The heritage line operates on most Sundays and Bank Holidays between April and September and selected Saturdays in midsummer. The railway hosts two apprenticeship schemes for permanent way and civil engineering training.

In 2003, today's East Kent Railway became a charitable trust.

*Visit www.eastkentrailway.co.uk for more details.

Class 142 Pacer No. 142017 which arrived on the East Kent Railway in the summer of 2020 is seen during a training exercise. Soon be joined by its stablemate No. 142036, it will be used for driver experience sessions and private hire trips. EKR

Edge Hill 'Terrier' 0-6-0T No.2 (formerly No.74 Shadwell), with brake van No.2. Left to rot for years after the end of a short-lived industrial dream, only the bicycle in the picture ever ran again. CSRM

Manning Wardle 0-4-0ST No. 1088 *Sankey* at Edge Hill in June 1922, with construction foreman John Brenchley, a Colonel Stephens employee, on the footplate. CSRM

EDGE HILL LIGHT RAILWAY: THE ULTIMATE 'DEAD DUCK!'

Edge Hill, an escarpment in the parish of Ratley and Upton in Warwickshire, is best known as the setting for the first battle of the English Civil War.

The Royalist forces of King Charles I and the Parliamentarian army commanded by the Earl of Essex clashed here on Sunday, October 23, 1642. The battle proved inconclusive, with both sides claiming victory.

The following year, after reports published by printer Thomas Jackson that two ghostly armies had been seen fighting in the sky, the King sent a royal commission to visit the site.

Three centuries later Edge Hill again became a graveyard, with the ghostly remains being those of a railway which many people believe never should have been built.

Just like the battle, the outcome of the Edge Hill Light Railway (EHLR) remained very much unfinished business. Its construction was suspended with such apparent haste that after a lapse of several years the mechanical excavator that has been used to build it was still to be found with its grab half-raised to load a bucketful of earth.

This 3½-mile line was promoted in association with the Stratford-upon-Avon & Midland Junction Railway (SMJR), which was formed in 1909 by the merger of three earlier companies: the East and West Junction Railway, the Evesham, Redditch & Stratford-upon-Avon Junction Railway, and the Stratford-upon-Avon, Towcester, & Midland Junction Railway.

In 1910 the Northampton and Banbury Junction Railway was purchased and an east-west network was formed which linked routes to Bedford and Northampton in the east to lines leading towards Banbury and Gloucester in the west, via Towcester and Stratford.

The three constituent railways had each been built with a view to carrying Northamptonshire iron ore to South Wales and the West Midlands, but they were all unable to finance their planned lines in full. The formation of the SMJR in 1909 was in effect a financial reconstruction, but the management of the combined company also showed a certain flair for generating

tourist income, based on the connection with Shakespeare and also the family connections with George Washington. Furthermore, the line was developed as a shorter route for Midland Railway goods traffic from the Bristol area to London.

John Brenchley by the track on the summit in June 1922. CSRM

THE EHLR had its origin in the opening-up of the rich ironstone deposits which have been known for many centuries to exist in this part of the South Midlands. First World War requirements intensified the demand for British ironstone and the EHLR was promoted as a means of tapping into those deposits which exist in the immediate vicinity of Edge Hill.

An application was submitted for a Light Railway Order for a standard gauge line five miles and 58 chains long, from a junction with the SMR at Burton Dassett sidings to Nadbury Camp and Sunrising on the top of Edge Hill. It was stated that 'great developments' were anticipated as a result of ready access to the ironstone field.

However, the fact that the line was not opened until after the cessation of hostilities, when the changed economic conditions occasioned a gradually lessening demand for British ore, may have considerably hastened the fate which ultimately befell it.

Two of the initial directors of the light railway were also those of two related Black Country iron companies: T&I Bradley of Bilston and T&I Bradley & Son on Darlaston. They established an owning company for both the ironstone and the light rails as the Banbury Ironstone Co Ltd. Its chairman in 1922 was Harry Willmott, who was also chairman of the SMJR, and the chief officers of the light railway were also those of the main line company.

The promoters acquired mineral rights to more than 600 acres of land around Edge Hill.

The company could have opted to build a basic mineral railway, but instead chose a fully-fledged public light railway. And who did they choose as its engineer? Colonel Stephens.

The incline: designed by Colonel Stephens, it was the biggest feature of engineering on the Edge Hill Light Railway, as seen in 1935. To the left are the linesman's hut and the spur line to the locomotive water reservoir. CSRM

A SHORT REIGN AND RAILWAY

Recently released from his army commitments, Stephens had previously had dealings with Willmott during a brief spell on the Isle of Wight Central Railway as engineer and locomotive superintendent in 1911 before he was ousted from there by Willmott's son Russell.

Plans for the EHLR were drawn up by Stephens' office in Tonbridge and his initial proposal was to tackle the 300ft escarpment by starting out at Fenny Compton and building up the slope to lessen the gradients, but this was shown to be too expensive.

The second plan involved an 11¼-mile railway from a triangular junction with the SMJR at Burton Dassett. Two miles up the line, a rope-worked incline could have led to three branches accessing separate parts of the ore field.

A public inquiry into the LRO application was conducted in November 1917 by the Light Railway Commissioners. It led to the planned line being cut back to just 5½ miles, with the SM JR having running powers to the foot of the cable-worked incline; passengers might be carried over this two-mile section, it was conjectured.

The LRO order was approved on July 17, 1918, but early in 1919 Stephens seemed to have stood down as engineer. History repeated itself and he was replaced by Russell Willmott. Maybe the promoters of the EHLR has merely used Stephens for his expertise and skills to obtain the LRO, without actually wanting to have him managing the project.

However, the purchase of two second-hand locomotives to work the line had all the hallmarks to the colonel. Both were 1872-built LBSCR 'Terrier' 0-6-0Ts and the first to arrive, in 1919, was No. 673 *Deptford*, which became EHLR No.1. It was followed a year later by No. 674 *Shadwell*, which became No. 2. The

Edge Hill Light Railway 'Terrier' 0-6-0T No. 1 in open storage in 1931. THE RAILWAY MAGAZINE

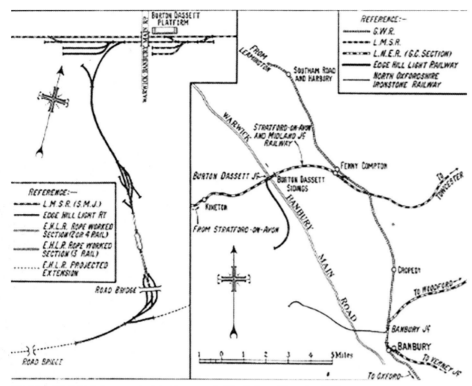

The Edge Hill Light Railway as depicted by a map in *The Railway Magazine*, 1931.

'Terriers' were used to work the EHLR's low-level line.

The EHLR had no engine shed in which to keep them, although there was a turntable at the junction. The pair were serviced and mainly kept at the SMJR's Stratford-upon-Avon locomotive shed, under an agreement made by the two companies' shared chief officers. In return, the SMJR is said to have used one of the 'Terriers' for its Stratford to Broom Junction trains when it was short of traction.

The only other examples of main line stock were two Great Eastern Railway ex-Army brake vans.

Building of the line began in 1919 but progress was very slow, and indeed may have been suspended for a time. This may have been because the post-war industrial boom was ending, accompanied by a perceived reduced demand for iron ore. Also, the Grouping of 1923 was on the horizon, with the SMJR due to become part of the new London, Midland & Scottish Railway, and the EHLR directors fearing that their investment would mature sooner than planned.

RAILWAY CUT SHORT
Russell Willmott died from cancer at his home in Newport on the Isle of Wight on June 20 and was replaced by consulting engineer Edgar Ferguson, who at the age of 74 had by then all but retired from main line railway assignments. However, he did have experience of light railway engineering and he may have had a hand in the post-Stephens developments at Edge Hill including the incline mechanisms.

Some ironstone trains had been running by the time that the half-mile gravity worked or 'self acting' 1-in-9 incline was completed in summer 1922. The first 250 yards of the incline was single track followed by a double-line loop, which in turn merged into a three-rail formation in which the centre rail was common to trains in both directions.

The ground at the top of the ridge through which the line was being built was ironstone. The trains were said to have carried 60 tons a day and the ore was sent for onward transportation for smelting in the Midlands.

As laid out, the EHLR ran starting from a small yard which hitherto had been used for other ironstone workings, next to the SMJR's Burton Dassett platform on the Banbury to Warwick Road. Slight gradients took it around 2½ miles to a fan of sorting sidings at the foot of the cable-worked incline, at the top of which the line ran for a very short distance to finish at an uncompleted cutting near the road to Ratley village. Also, there was a back shunt from the incline top and a few yards of track towards Nadbury.

The railway obtained small Manning Wardle 0-4-0ST No. 1088 of 1888 *Sankey* from its original employment on the building of the Manchester Ship Canal, from Topham Jones and Co (who had built the Oxfordshire Ironstone line), in June 1922.

However, disaster struck on Tuesday, October 10, 1922, when the directors decided to inspect the incline mechanisms. In charge of running a rake of wagons was ganger John Brenchley, who had worked for Stephens as a construction hand on the East Kent Light Railway.

The rake ran away and ploughed into the sand drag at the bottom and the wagons on the counterbalancing rake came hurtling over the top. They struck Edgar Ferguson a glancing blow which proved fatal.

The incline was not repaired and commercial traffic on the line ceased, although there is a record of an ore load from the Edge Hill quarries at Burton Dassett yard on January 27, 1925. One man was employed by the EHLR as a caretaker from 1922 until 1937, but carried out no maintenance.

DERELICTION, DECAY AND DEATH
An article in *The Railway Magazine* in April 1931 found that all three locomotives were standing derelict on the railway; the 'Terriers' were "partially covered with tarpaulins and in quite good repair considering that they have been for five years exposed to wind and weather."

It added: "Although the locomotives and rolling-stock are still in good condition considering the ordeal to which they have been exposed, time and weather have played sad havoc with the permanent way, which in several places is almost buried under falls of earth and subsidences of the cutting walls.

"Generally, however, the line does not give the impression of having been left derelict for nearly five years, and no doubt it could easily be reopened should such a fortunate eventuality be made possible by future trade developments."

That reopening would never materialise.

Early on during the Second World War, consideration was given to the resurrection of the EHLR, but the nearby Oxfordshire Ironstone line was considered adequate.

In the autumn of 1941, the track from the lower part of the EHLR was requisitioned for the building of a vast military depot at Long Marston off the Stratford to Cheltenham line near Honeybourne. The track and the associated earthworks had been removed by June 1942.

The locomotives were therefore left isolated and unable to run to the SMJR. A visitor to the site on July 8, 1945, recorded: "At the foot of the incline stood two 'Terrier' 0-6-0Ts. On the left hand side of No. 674, EHLR. 2 had been painted above the LBSCR lettering in white paint, but no such lettering was visible on No. 673.

"No. 673 was fitted with an extended smoke-box, while No. 674 still retained its original shorter boiler. Most of the cab fittings on both locos had been removed, with the exception of the regulator handles, brake levers, sanding and damper control levers. The general condition of both locos was very poor, being almost entirely covered with rust, and it is certain that they will not be of any further use except as scrap.

"The wagons are mostly in a most dilapidated condition, one or two being almost intact, but the remainder broken up, with their sides and wheels spread all around."

The stock might well have been cut up early during the war's desperate early years but by 1943, the United States had entered the conflict, bringing with it vast amounts of military hardware from across the Atlantic. Scrap metal was therefore no longer at a premium.

However, Britain was left bankrupt after the war ended and scrap was again in high demand.

James Friswell & Son of Banbury cut up the locomotives during the spring and summer of 1946. Those real-life ghosts of Edge Hill had finally be exorcised.

So ended one of the shortest-lived standard gauge railways anywhere. It is often said it hindsight that this or that railway line should never have been built,

and this one must be a prime example if not the definitive article.

Due to a sharp decline in patronage, the SMJR lost its passenger services between June 1957 and April 1952. The South Wales ironstone traffic also declined and the severe operational

constraints on the SMJR led to the diversion of traffic to other routes in 1964. The route was closed on July 5, 1965, except for the section between Burton Dassett sidings and Fenny Compton which remains open to service the Ministry of Defence establishment at Kineton.

Rusting merrily away, Manning Wardle 0-4-0ST No. 1088 *Sankey* is parked permanently under Camp Lane bridge, as seen in 1935. CSRM

The northern end of the Edgehill escarpment at Knowle End. The trees to the immediate left of the white house in the distance mark the line of the Edge Hill Light Railway (EHLR) which ran up to the top of the hill via a rope-powered 1-in-6 incline at that point. NIGEL MYKURA*

Chapter 12

Kerr Stuart Skylark class 0-4-2T No. 802 of 1902 outside Snailbeach shed, with another locomotive visible within and the remains of a third to one side. CSRM

Class 10-12-D 4-6-0Ts were built by the Baldwin Locomotive Works in Philadelphia for the British War Department Light Railways. They were destined for service in France during the First World War. After the conflict ended, many were sold and went on to work in France, Britain and India. No. 778 worked in India until the 1980s, finishing at the Upper India Sugar Mills in Uttar Pradesh. Repatriated, it was restored by the Greensand Railway Museum Trust at the Leighton Buzzard Railway and entered service there in August 2007. The completion of the restoration made No. 778, sister to three locomotives which worked on the Snailbeach District Railways, the first Class 10-12-D to operate in Britain since the 1940s. It is seen in action on September 13, 2014, during the Tracks to the Trenches First World War-themed event at the Apedale Valley Light Railway in the Potteries. ROBIN JONES

SNAILBEACH DISTRICT RAILWAYS –
A LEAD BALLOON

This narrow-gauge mining line had a somewhat longer life span than the Edge Hill Light Railway, but both its fortunes and survival were inextricably linked to the minerals market.

The Snailbeach District Railways Company was incorporated by an Act of Parliament on August 5, 1873. The purpose of the railway was to carry lead ore from mines on the western flank of the Stiperstones, a landmark ridge of rock, three miles to Pontesbury. Here the ore was transferred to the Great Western Railway and London & North Western Railway's joint Minsterley branch.

The line was built to the rare gauge of 2ft 4in and ended at Snailbeach, the location of Shropshire's largest and richest lead mine. There the station was variously known as Crowsnest, Snailbeach station or Snailbeach wharf. From Crowsnest, a reverse branch ran

on a 1-in-25 gradient to Snailbeach lead mine, where the locomotive shed was built.

There had been an initial plan to extend it by a further two miles, which would have brought it closer to more lead mines at Pennerley. An extension to Tankerville also was considered but neither was proceeded with. It was originally hoped that the line would carry passengers as a fully-fledged public railway, but it never became anything more than a private mineral line.

The railway was engineered by Henry Dennis who had performed a similar role for the 2ft 4¼in gauge Glyn Valley Railway. Dennis hired contractor Elias Griffiths, who had built the Glyn Valley

Tramway, and work began in August 1875. The line opened in 1877.

There was an uninterrupted gradient of 1-in-37 from Pontesbury to Crowsnest, and roads were crossed by bridges rather that level crossings. As such, like the Festiniog Railway, it was ideally

The restored former locomotive shed with narrow gauge rails still in place on April 26, 2017. RICHARD SZWEJKOWSKI*

Four hopper wagons on the elevated unloading stage at the Pontesbury transfer sidings. CSRM

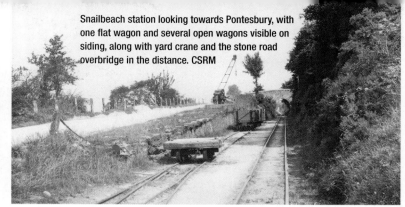

Snailbeach station looking towards Pontesbury, with one flat wagon and several open wagons visible on siding, along with yard crane and the stone road overbridge in the distance. CSRM

Snailbeach shed with locomotive No.4 (Baldwin 4-6-0T No.44522) in October 1938. Stiperstones mine is in the background. CSRM

The terminus at Pontesbury with a flat wagon, a open wagon, the tarring plant and various other buildings and structures. CSRM

Locomotive No.4 on the bridge at Pontesbury over the Shrewsbury to Minsterly road on April 25, 1940. CSRM

suited for gravity working of outward laden mineral trains, with locomotives used to haul the empty wagons back up. Incoming traffic consisted of coal for the mines' pumping engines and processing plant.

Despite the fact that the line was severely short of capital from the outset, it was nonetheless prosperous at first, carrying 14,000 tons of minerals a year and paying a 3% dividend. However, in 1884, the Tankerville Great Consols Company mine, the largest user of the railway, closed and tonnage fell to 5500 tons – halving the railway's traffic.

Trade slumped in the ensuing years to the extent that closure of the railway was considered in 1892 and an attempt was made to sell it.

Henry Dennis and his family made strenuous efforts to revive the railway just before the turn of the century. However, the early Edwardian period saw a slump in lead prices and no profit could be made. Output fell to just 500 tons in 1905.

While lead ore ceased to be the mainstay of the line, Dennis built up a new traffic in processing Snailbeach mine waste and roadstone, and ensured that the railway was solvent before he died in 1906. He was succeeded as railway chairman by his son H Dyke Dennis.

The family had promoted a stone quarry, the Granhams Moor Quarry at Eastridge, with William Toye, a local businessman and in 1905 a branch was built to serve it. An extra locomotive was required and so 0-4-2T *Sir Theodore* was borrowed from the Glyn Valley Tramway. However the slight difference in gauge made it too wide for the track and it was returned unused. Instead a new locomotive, WG Bagnall 0-6-0T No. 1797 of 1906 *Dennis* was bought and it became the line's No.1.

Freight peaked in 1909, when 38,000 tons were carried, but demand dwindled again during the First World War. By 1920 there was virtually no traffic; the line's sole locomotive was out of use and it became reliant on gravity working and horse power.

THE COLONEL TO THE RESCUE

It was around this time that the Snailbeach District Railways came to the attention of Colonel Stephens and his friends including J C White and H Montague, and in 1920 they began negotiations to acquire the ailing line.

The colonel took over the railway company in December

Basic map of the Snailbeach District Railways. GWERNOL*

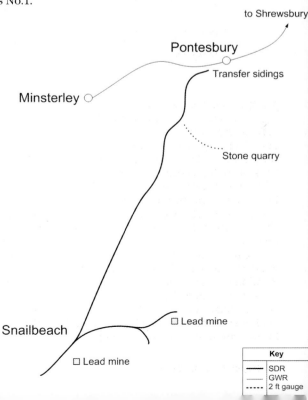

to Shrewsbury

Pontesbury

Transfer sidings

Minsterley

Stone quarry

Snailbeach

☐ Lead mine

☐ Lead mine

Key	
	SDR
	GWR
	2 ft gauge

A view of the remaining mine buildings at Snailbeach on April 26, 2017. RICHARD SZWEJKOWSKI*

The quartzite rock ride of the Stiperstones towered above the Snailbeach District Railways. At 1759ft above sea level, it is the second-highest hill in the county, surpassed only by Brown Clee Hill at 1772ft. KAT DODD*

His third locomotive was Kerr Stuart Skylark class 0-4-2T No. 802 of 1902.

Stephens also found that the Snailbeach wagon fleet was badly worn out and only 12 could run. He initiated the repair of 16 derelict wagons and bought several War Department C class bogie wagons.

Initial traffic and receipts proved disappointing despite these improvements, but within a few years Stephens had turned the line's fortunes around. Until 1928, much of the traffic consisted of barytes from the reprocessed quarry waste from Snailbeach mine, and material from the Crowsnest mine tailings.

The year before, Haywards' Quarries had opened a new roadstone quarry at Callow Hill and this brought a new prosperity to the railway. Stephens looked at starting a passenger service and went so far as to consider suitable carriages, but again, it did not happen.

Shropshire County County took over Callow Hill Quarry in 1931 to tap the high-grade Ordovician siltstone. The crushed stone was loaded into wagons which ran by gravity to nearby Pontesbury, where the council set up a tarring plant.

Also, traffic from the Gavel Trading Company at Snailbeach ensured another income stream throughout the Thirties.

An adit into the mine at Snailbeach with the remains of the narrow gauge track that ran into it. RICHARD SZWEJKOWSKI*

1922, in effect buying it almost as if it was his personal property.

He brought in consignments of second-hand standard gauge railway sleepers, cut them if half and used them to replace the rotting Snailbeach ones. He then relaid the line with 45lb rail.

Stephens brought in three former government locomotives to run it. In 1923 he acquired a pair of War Department US-built Baldwin 10-12-D 4-6-0Ts that had been supplied to the War Department Light Railways for use on the trench railways of the Western Front. They were No. 44383 of 1916, and No 44522 of 1917, and became Snailbeach's Nos. 3 and 4 respectively. The pair were from a batch refurbishment by Bagnall after war damage. The colonel also introduced the type to the Ashover Light Railway and Welsh Highland Railway.

Surviving track of the Snailbeach District Railways as seen on April 26, 2017. RICHARD SZWEJKOWSKI*

SNAILBEACH AFTER STEPHENS

After Stephens died on October 23, 1931, his long-time deputy William Austen took over as engineer, manager and part-owner. He then tried in vain to sell the railway to the county council.

He brought in two retired railwaymen to help him run the line, who had also assisted him on the Shropshire & Montgomeryshire Railway. John Pike, the former goods commercial manager with the LMS, became the Snailbeach chairman, and James Ramsey, who had been goods and mineral plant superintendent of the Caledonian Railway, joined the company board.

The marginal profitability of the line vanished with the Second World War, when the council reduced road repairs. Indeed, traffic fell by half.

Gravel Trading closed and dismantled its Snailbeach equipment in March 1944. By then, there was virtually no traffic on the upper part of the line but it had to remain open as the locomotive shed was at Snailbeach.

The loss-making line faced closure again in February 1946, and asked the county council for help. A body blow was dealt by a boiler inspector who failed all three operational locomotives in 1946, leaving the line without motive power. The short-term remedy was to hire an agricultural tractor to haul empty wagons back up the Callow Hill quarry, and it started work in July 1946. April 14, 1947, saw the council lease the Pontesbury to Callow Hill section and effectively become the sole operator of the line, continuing to use tractors.

The three locomotives were cut up at Snailbeach by TW Ward in 1950 and the line between there and Callow Hill was lifted soon afterwards. The railway finally closed in 1959, the last railway equipment being scrapped in 1961. The revived Talyllyn Railway purchased the remaining track in 1962.

The quarry remained open but the railway was lifted and, between Callow Hill and the road bridge at Pontesbury, converted into a road. The council ran its lorries along this road and paid rent to the railway company. As lorries became larger the long single-track road from Callow Lane to the quarry became impractical and was closed. A new access road was built in 1998 from the A488 at Pontesbury to the quarry at Callow Hill, when the quarry was extended and deepened.

The council sold the quarry to Tarmac plc in 2003, but by 2006 most heavy machinery had been removed. Quarrying permission existed until 2013. .

The railway company remains in existence, though it was offered for sale for around £25,000 in 1984. The only parts that were sold were the Callow Hill quarry and the trackbed from Pontesbury

The locomotive shed with a restored wagon and tractor, the form of motive power in the latter years, after the Baldwin Class 10-12-D 4-6-0Ts were worn out. RICHARD SZWEJKOWSKI*

Remains of the 'main line' of the Snailbeach District Railways. The bridge parapets which remain carried rails to the mine tailings tip. RICHARD SZWEJKOWSKI*

The front of the surviving engine shed. RICHARD SZWEJKOWSKI*

through to Callow Lane, plus a small section of land that was sold to private purchasers at Snailbeach (near Prospect House and Cottages) and the Crowsnest terminal.

Artefacts of the old railway can still be seen, mainly in Snailbeach, where the engine shed has been restored and rails remain in place on the lines leading to the old mines, and a tractor and reconstructed original hopper wagon are available for inspection.

There was internet talk of the line's revival as a heritage railway in 2007, but nothing happened.

Chapter 13

Large England 0-4-0TT *Welsh Pony* raring to go on June 27, 2020, during the 'virtual test steaming' made necessary by Covid-19. CHRIS PARRY

FFESTINIOG & WELSH HIGHLAND RAILWAYS

When Colonel Stephens was appointed to run two classic narrow gauge lines in North Wales, he faced an uphill battle against rising competition from road transport and low investment. However, both lines were reborn in the heritage era and have more than exceeded the tourist expectations of the era of Stephens and his assistant William Austen.

More than 27,000 people around the world watched a test run of one of Britain's great classic narrow gauge locomotives – one that had not steamed for 80 years – on Saturday, June 27, 2020.

Did the rebirth of the Ffestiniog Railway's George England 0-4-0STT No. 5 *Welsh Pony* in the line's fabled Boston Lodge Works set a new record?

Sadly not; the Covid-19 pandemic meant most were watching on their computer screens via lineside video cameras. Only a handful were physically present, including the railway's regular minister Dr Richard Buxton who lives in near Porthmadog, and was born in 1980, the last year that *Welsh Pony* ran!

There had never been another locomotive relaunch quite like it. The culmination of a restoration project that cost in excess of £250,000 was broadcast

online in three episodes: the lighting up at 10am by Millie Lewin, daughter of Ffestiniog & Welsh Highland Railways general manager Paul Lewin; the first whistle being sounded at 1pm and at 4pm the sight of the locomotive moving under its own steam for the first time. Old timber that had once formed part of *Welsh Pony's* boiler cladding had been used to light the fire.

The first run of *Welsh Pony* in the 21st century was the latest instalment in a story that had begun in 1863. In the previous decade, it had become clear that the horse-drawn and gravity-worked slate carrying line was reaching its operational capacity, while the Blaenau Ffestiniog slate quarries were producing more stone. The railway therefore investigated

A poster designed to encourage tourists to the Welsh Highland Railway. Ff&WHR ARCHIVES

the possibility of introducing steam locomotives to increase its carrying capacity. While narrow gauge steam locomotives had been tried before, very few had been built to such a narrow gauge.

The company invited manufacturers to tender to build the line's first locomotives in 1862. The bid of George England and Co of Hatcham Iron Works in New Cross, Surrey, was duly accepted in February of the following year and four side tank engines were supplied to the Festiniog in 1863/64. No. 1 *Princess*, No. 2 *Prince*, No. 3 *Mountaineer* and No. 4 *Palmerston* were the first successful 1ft 11½in gauge engines to be built commercially. All but *Mountaineer* survive today, *Prince* and *Palmerston* having been returning to running order in the preservation era.

Traffic on the FR had outgrown the capabilities of the four original 'Small Englands' by 1867 and Charles Easton Spooner, the line's the secretary and engineer from 1856-86, had drawn up a revised specification for a new engine, which he took to George England.

The larger and improved design with saddle tanks, a longer wheelbase and larger driving wheels became known as the 'Large England' class. Just two examples were built, with *Welsh Pony* and *Little Giant* being delivered in 1867.

Welsh Pony worked, with minor overhauls, until 1891 when most of its components were replaced and an overall cab fitted. In 1915 a new boiler was fitted and underwent a substantial overhaul for most of 1929. *Little Giant* was withdrawn in 1932 and cannibalised for spares, but *Welsh Pony* was run until February 1940, despite it being officially withdrawn the year before.

Early in the heritage era, it had been intended to restore *Welsh Pony*, but separate matters including the arrival of Hunslet 2-4-0TTs *Linda* and *Blanche* from the closed Penrhyn Railway kept it from the top of the queue.

Welsh Pony was repainted red in 1984 and plinthed outside Porthmadog Harbour station where it remained until 2002. It was then moved to Glan y Pwll shed. In 2013, members voted to restore it, and the project began the following year.

Both it and the Ffestiniog Railway may well owe their survival to a man who took over as engineer in 1923 and was later the company's chairman and managing director. He would have been familiar with *Welsh Pony* and its stablemates and would most likely have ridden behind it. His management skills, introduced at a time that the railway was

Welsh Pony storms back into Boston Lodge Works on a short test run on June 27, 2020. Ff&WHR

going into decline, may well have saved it from premature closure. Had that happened, it is unlikely what we would today have the magnificent world-leading heritage operation that is the Ffestiniog & Welsh Highland Railways today. His name? Colonel Holman F Stephens.

THE FESTINIOG AND ITS 'FIRSTS'
The Festiniog Railway was conceived nearly four decades before Stephens was born. Landowner William Alexander

Madocks (1773-1828) not only gave his name to the town of Porthmadog (Portmadoc) at the western end of this legendary mountain line, and the neighbouring settlement of Tremadog (Tremadoc), but also created them. His aim was to turn around the fortunes of a very impoverished part of North Wales by improving road and rail links and introducing manufacture.

He promoted local turnpike roads in the area, and built a great embankment across Traeth Mawr, the estuary of the Afon Glaslyn, eliminating both a dangerous tidal crossing and a circuitous detour that had kept much of the locality in relative isolation.

This embankment was completed in 1811 and became known as the Cob. It was intended to form part of a great rail link running across central Wales to Porth Dinllaen on the Lleyn Peninsula.

The workmen who built the Cob were housed in a building at its eastern end which Madocks, as MP for Boston in Lincolnshire, named Boston Lodge. It

The classic view of original Festiniog double Fairlie *Little Wonder* hauling a mixed train of slate wagons and passenger coaches across the great embankment at Creuau Bank in 1871. Ff&WHR ARCHIVES

later became the railway's workshops, now the oldest of their type in the world still used as originally intended.

In 1821 he obtained an Act of Parliament for a harbour at Ynys y Tywyn, to be renamed Port Madoc. It took off as a harbour through which millions of tons of Snowdonian slate would be exported. He also surveyed routes for a horse-drawn railway to connect his harbour to the new but then small slate quarries at Blaenau Ffestiniog, from where the stone was taken by pack animal and farm carts over rough roads down to the River Dwyryd for onward transhipment by river boats and then sea-going sailing ships – a costly and time-consuming exercise.

Two years after Madocks' death in Paris, Samuel Holland, who was quarrying slate at Rhiw, and Henry Archer, a businessman from Dublin, promoted the building of the Festiniog Railway, which was incorporated by Act of Parliament on May 23, 1832.

Despite the switch to the Welsh spelling of Ffestiniog in recent times, the railway company – the oldest surviving one in the world – is correctly known as the Festiniog Railway Company because the anglicised spelling is the official title as defined by the Act. In this text, I am using the spelling that is appropriate to the time.

Worcestershire engineer James Spooner (the father of the abovementioned Charles Spooner) was engaged as both surveyor and builder of the railway, which he designed on a continuous slope averaging 1-in-80, so that the loaded slate wagons at Blaenau could run by gravity via the Cob down to the harbour at Porthmadog 13½ miles away. The line was constructed between 1833-36 to 1ft 11½in gauge, similar to the tramways being used in the slate quarries, and narrow enough to allow the railway to twist and turn through the mountains it had to climb. The narrow gauge also led to smaller wagons, which had the advantage of being easier to handle at the harbour.

In the wake of the success of Stephenson's Rocket at the Liverpool & Manchester Railway's Rainhill Trials of 1829, steam finally replaced horse traction in the vision of the future for transport. Yet not only was it thought impractical to run steam engines on so narrow a gauge, but carrying passengers on new lines built to less than the British standard gauge of 4ft 8½in was illegal. Nevertheless, there were tales of tourists being unofficially carried around 1850.

So the steam age passed the Festiniog by for nearly three decades, despite the booming quarry industry turning Blaenau into the slate capital of Wales.

Following the delivery of the abovementioned 'Small England' locomotives, the Board of Trade approved the running of passenger trains of the Festiniog – the first on a UK narrow gauge line. Four-wheeled carriages were built to accommodate visitors and provide a cheap service to quarrymen.

In 1869 the line's first double Fairlie articulated locomotive was introduced, and these double-ended machines have since become an internationally-recognised trademark of today's Ffestiniog. Robert Francis Fairlie, a longtime business associate of George England, held the view that conventional locomotive design was seriously deficient, because weight was wasted on unpowered wheels and on a tender that did nothing but carry fuel and water without contributing to the locomotive's adhesive weight. Furthermore, 'normal' locomotives had a quite different front and rear, and were not intended to be driven backwards for long periods, making the regular use of turntables necessary.

Fairlie's solution answer was to have a double-ended locomotive, one which carried all its fuel and water aboard and had every axle driven. His locomotives would have twin boilers joined back-to-back at the firebox ends, with the smokeboxes at each end, and controls at both ends of a central cab to allow the engine to be driven equally well in either direction.

Fairlie's first double-ended locomotive, *Pioneer*, was built by James Cross & Co of St Helens for the standard gauge Neath & Brecon Railway in 1865, but it was not successful.

It was a different story altogether on the Festiniog, for which double Fairlie 0-4-0+0-4-0T *Little Wonder* was built by England in 1869. The following February, Fairlie invited locomotive engineers from as far away as Russia, Mexico, Turkey and Sweden to Snowdonia to see his invention in action. His promotional exercise was a resounding success as it left him with orders for his double-ended engines flooding in. By 1876, 43 different railways round the world had operated his engines, which were most successful in the long term in Mexico and New Zealand.

His demonstration also proved once and for all that narrow gauge steam was a credible alternative to standard gauge steam in upland terrain.

The Festiniog's second double Fairlie was No. 8 *James Spooner*, supplied by Avonside in 1872. A third, No. 10 *Merddin Emrys* was delivered in 1879 and a fourth, No. 11 *Livingston Thompson* was built at Boston Lodge Works in 1886.

Fairlie also produced 'single' versions, resembling 'normal' locomotives. Effectively a double Fairlie cut in half, they had a single articulated power bogie combined with an unpowered bogie under the cab, maintaining the ability to negotiate sharp turns. Fairlie gave the Festiniog Railway Company a perpetual licence to use the Fairlie locomotive patent without restriction in return for using the line to demonstrate *Little Wonder*.

The Festiniog claimed another 'first' in 1872 when it introduced the first bogie carriages to operate in Britain, Nos 15 and 16. They were also the first iron-framed bogie coaches in the world. The continuous vacuum brake was installed in 1893, while electric train staff instruments were introduced in 1912.

Tourism had first been mentioned in the London & North Western Railway's Tourist Guide for 1876, extolling the virtues of a trip along the scenic Festiniog, illustrating it with a drawing of a lady in Welsh national dress riding on a narrow gauge train. The summer timetable for 1900 included nine trains daily each way, with journey times speeded up to an hour.

A classic Stephens view sees England 0-4-0STT *Palmerston* at Waenfawr on the Welsh Highland Railway with Festiniog coaching stock in 1924. Ff&WHR ARCHIVES

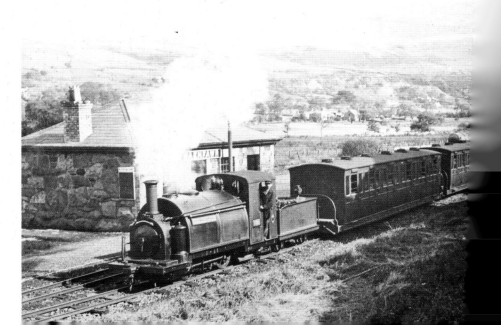

THE COMING OF THE WELSH HIGHLAND

The Festiniog's Charles Easton Spooner, who also owned a quarry at Bryngwyn, drew up a plan for a 60-mile narrow gauge network covering a vast area of North Wales between Pwllheli, Betws-y-Coed and Corwen.

Only two of his North Wales Narrow Gauge Railways lines were built. The first line to be constructed ran from Dinas to Bryngwyn five miles away, and opened in 1887.

The second line was in effect a continuation of the first, linked to it at Tryfan Junction. It ran up to lofty Rhyd Ddu, where a station first named Snowdon was built, and opened in 1881. It also served the slate quarries at Bryngwyn and Glan yr afon. While freight over the whole route was transferred to standard gauge wagons at Dinas Junction for the short trip to Caernarfon, the new railway did its utmost to attract late Victorian tourists to Snowdon, advertising itself as the line that was closest to the summit.

In 1901, the Portmadoc, Beddgelert & South Snowdon Railway obtained an Act of Parliament to take over the separate Croesor Tramway and extend it to Nant Gwynant via Beddgelert and the South Snowdon slate quarry, but as an electric rather than steam-powered line.

Building of the Portmadoc, Beddgelert & South Snowdon Railway began in the Aberglaslyn Pass in 1905. It took over power earlier obtained by the North Wales Narrow Gauge Railways to extend to Beddgelert in 1900. A new Hunslet 2-6-2T *Russell* was bought to help keep the by-then-ailing North Wales Narrow Gauge Railways operating until it too could be electrified and the two lines joined.

However, finances ran out and the series of tunnels planned for the eastern slopes of the Aberglaslyn Pass was abandoned. Regarding the plans for the electric railway, only the power station was built and it is still operating today.

The Croesor Tramway and North Wales Narrow Gauge Railways soldiered on, although passenger services over the latter ceased during the First World War.

The benefits of a through railway across Snowdonia was not lost on local councils however and in 1914 a Light Railway Order was promoted to take over both the North Wales Narrow Gauge Railways and Portmadoc, Beddgelert & South Snowdon Railway and complete the route. It came to nothing due to the advent of the First World War but it has been said that an expert in such matters was spotted in North Wales in 1918 and may have been waiting for his opportunity – Colonel Stephens.

The idea of the trans-Snowdonian line was revived in 1920 by Henry Joseph

Russell brings a Welsh Highland Railway brake carriage into Porthmadog Harbour station. Ff&WHR ARCHIVES

Jack, managing director of Aluminium Corporation based at Dolgarrog in the Conwy Valley, who by then had taken control of both the North Wales Narrow Gauge Railways and the Portmadoc, Beddgelert & South Snowdon Railway, together with two local politicians and Scottish distillery owner Sir John Henderson Stewart. In July 1921, Stewart gained control of the Festiniog to obtain extra rolling stock for this new line.

The Aluminium Corporation obtained a Light Railway Order to build what would be known as the Welsh Highland Railway in 1922, incorporating the routes of both of the lines it had acquired.

The Welsh Highland Railway would run from Dinas Junction to Porthmadog, where it would run through the town and join the Festiniog Railway at Harbour station, crossing the Cambrian Railways (later Great Western) Pwllheli line via the Croesor Tramway flat crossing.

Alfred McAlpine & Sons was handed the contract to upgrade both the Croesor Tramway and the North Wales Narrow

Gauge Railways and build the linking section between Rhyd Ddu and Croesor Junction, thereby completing the long-dreamed-of through route. It has been rumoured that Stephens had been involved in laying out the new line in the section through Beddgelert.

The North Wales Narrow Gauge Railways section which had closed to passengers in 1916 was reopened on July 31, 1922, and the completed Welsh Highland Railway was opened on June 1, 1923. The two remaining North Wales Narrow Gauge Railways locomotives, *Russell* and single Fairlie 0-6-4T *Moel Tryfan*, were joined by US-built War Department Baldwin 4-6-0T No. 590, one of several which had seen service during the war and were afterwards sold privately for use on narrow gauge lines both in Britain and overseas. The small fleet was bolstered by the Festiniog's England tanks – by then all having been converted from side to saddle tanks and carriages, while there were occasional ventures over the Welsh Highland by the double Fairlies from Porthmadog too.

Second-hand ex-War Department Baldwin 4-6-0T No. 590 waits to takes its Welsh Highland train bound for Beddgelert across Britannia Bridge in Porthmadog. Ff&WHR ARCHIVES

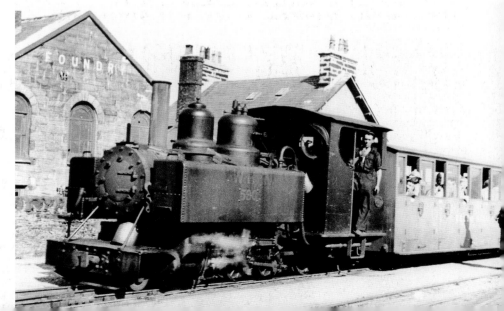

William Austen was in charge of the Festiniog and Welsh Highland railways after the death of Colonel Stephens in 1931. CSRM

THE COLONEL APPOINTED

As chairman, Henry Jack became the prime mover in the opening of the Welsh Highland. However, there were doubts by then about the viability of running a year-round passenger service. The management saw that the slate industry and the summer influx of tourist could keep the new line's head above water, but from 1920 onwards potential passengers were already turning to the new bus routes that would compete with it.

The fatal flaw in the scheme was that it was backed by loan funding from both the local authorities and the Ministry of Transport. The railway never earned enough money to repay the interest on these loans, and that prompted its ultimate downfall.

With the construction of the line by McAlpine due to be completed by the end of March 1923, a new engineer was needed – and Jack had the very man to hand.

Stephens was formally appointed as engineer on May 1 that year and working within its severely-limited budget he influenced the choice of equipment bought to run the line. Jack resigned in November 1924 after shareholders expressed misgivings at the financial results of the Welsh Highland.

Stephens was appointed chairman of both the Welsh Highland and Festiniog

Slate country spectacular: double Fairlie *Merddin Emrys* leaving Tan-y-Bwlch for Porthmadog in the 1930s. Ff&WHR ARCHIVES

on December 16, 1924. He became managing director the following March. The colonel had by then accrued a first-class track record in handling railways that needed to be run 'on the cheap' because they were short of capital. Even so, in Snowdonia he had his work cut out.

The Festiniog had slipped into a poor condition, compounded by old-fashioned working practices, and the Welsh Highland was blatantly under-resourced. Passenger levels were dropping off almost by the month, and soon there was no justification to run winter services.

Jack had suggested that Stephens used his railmotors, like those he had pioneered on the Kent & East Sussex as we saw in Chapter 4, but Stephens saw that the situation was already too far gone for that.

Through modern management techniques and methods of cost control Stephens and his successor William Austen were able to give the Festiniog and Welsh Highland railways new cause for hope – but it remained just that – hope. The pair halted and even partially reversed the Festiniog's deterioration, and probably saved it from closure, but both lines came to rely just as much on

summer tourists as the traditional life-blood quarry traffic.

Winter passenger services were discontinued on the Welsh Highland during the winter of 1924 due to poor traffic. A dispute with the Great Western Railway concerning the costs of the crossing over its line at Porthmadog also caused problems, despite it having been used since 1867 without any charges or problems. The railway even had to resort to escorting passengers over the crossing on foot.

The Welsh Highland was unable to pay debenture interest after 1923 and the county council sued in 1927, placing the railway in receivership. Services continued but by 1933 it was run down and the local authorities decided to close it. However, the following year the company agreed to lease the Welsh Highland to the Festiniog for 42 years. The Festiniog company attempted to change the line's fortunes by refocussing on the tourist market. This included painting the carriages in bright colours, including yellow and blue, and promoting the Aberglaslyn Pass as a destination.

The timing was fortunate and the railway was able to capitalise on the advent

This 1930s view sees double Fairlie *Merddin Emrys* waiting to cross the Britannia bridge linking the Festiniog and Welsh Highland railways. Ff&WHR ARCHIVES

Double Fairlie *Merddin Emrys* on a Down train at Minffordd in the 1930s. Ff&WHR ARCHIVES

of annual holidays, which brought visitors to the Welsh coast in droves, especially from the industrial conurbations of the Midlands and the North West. The Festiniog also tried to promote round trip journeys, with passengers taking the standard gauge line to Dinas, travelling on the Welsh Highland and the Festiniog to Blaenau and then changing again to take the standard gauge railway to their original starting point.

Yet such initiatives were not enough, especially during the Depression of the Thirties. The leasehold deal meant that the Festiniog would be forced to pay rent even if the Welsh Highland made a loss.

From March 24, 1930, all winter services the Festiniog also ended, including morning and evening quarrymen's services. Austen resigned in protest at the company's economies in 1936 as the Welsh Highland's losses continued. The last passenger service on the Welsh Highland ran on September 5 that year and the following year it ran its last freight train – becoming dormant even as the Festiniog continued to operate.

In 1941 the Welsh Highland's track was requisitioned for the war effort, with much of the rolling stock sold off. The Festiniog surrendered its lease in 1943 and, in exchange for £550 compensation, was allowed to keep Moel Tryfan. On January 22, 1944, the local county council petitioned the High Court for it to be wound up.

Before then, the outbreak of the Second World War had seen ordinary passenger services on the Festiniog itself come to an end, the last running on September 15, 1939, with the final workmen's train being run the following day. Slate trains were still operated three days each week, running 'as required' between Blaenau Ffestiniog and the Great Western Railway's Minffordd exchange sidings, but the gravity trains were finally discontinued. Meanwhile,

Festiniog Railway No. 5 *Welsh Pony* at Beddgelert during a foray up the sister Welsh Highland Railway in the 1930s. Ff&WHR ARCHIVES

the war killed off the Festiniog's promising tourist trade.

Slate traffic ended on August 1, 1946, and only the short section of the line from Duffws to the North Western main line railway yard through Blaenau Ffestiniog town centre continued in operation. It was leased to the quarry owners on October 7 that year, giving the all but defunct company and its resident manager at Porthmadog a very modest income.

However, the company was so short of money that it could not afford an Act of Parliament which would provide the statutory powers necessary to close the railway and lift it. Soon the line was very overgrown and in a severe state of decay.

With hindsight, it may well have been thanks to Stephens' and Austen's involvement that it lasted as long as it did, and future events would lead to its rebirth, and eventually, that of its much shorter-lived sister line.

THE REBIRTH OF THE FESTINIOG

History records that the world's first railway to be saved by enthusiast volunteers and reopened as an operating concern was the Talyllyn Railway. Saved largely at the instigation of transport author Tom Rolt, the newly-formed Talyllyn Railway Preservation Society ran its first service on May 14, 1951.

Around the same time however, there were also those who felt strongly that the Festiniog should not be allowed to pass into history. Teenager Leonard Heath-Humphreys' letter about the line's potential for restoration was published in the January 1951 edition of *Journal of the British Locomotive*.

Having devised the idea of a fighting fund to stop it from being lifted, in July 1950 Leonard had made contact with the Festiniog company and suggested launching a society to reopen it. His letter three months later prompted only two replies, but nonetheless provoked editorial comment in *Trains Illustrated* two months later. That generated 22 responses, and another 48 enthusiasts were 'drafted' into the scenario through subsequent letters by Leonard in the *Railway Gazette*, *The Engineer* and *Engineering*.

As a result of Leonard's initiative, on September 8, 1951, a public meeting was held by the Bristol Railway Circle, attended by just 12 people. There Leonard met Allan Garraway, a member of the Talyllyn society who was later to become the revived Festiniog's first full-time general manager, a position he was to hold until 1983.

A second meeting was arranged for October on the Old Bull public house in Barnet. A legal committee was set up and meetings were held with the FR company board during 1952, but progress was slow.

The big breakthrough came when businessman Alan Pegler attended a meeting of the nascent Festiniog Railway

Two double Fairlies at Porthmadog Harbour station in 1936. Ff&WHR ARCHIVES

The Ffestiniog Railway's vintage weekend of October 15/16, 2005, saw a unique line-up of six locomotives at Harbour station: England 0-4-0STTs No 2. *Prince*, No. 4 *Palmerston* and No. 5 *Welsh Pony*, double Fairlies No. 3 *Livingston Thompson*. No. 10 *Merddin Emrys* and No. 12 *David Lloyd George*. *Livingston Thompson* has never steamed on the line in the heritage era, and it was only in 2020 that *Welsh Pony* did. Ff&WHR ARCHIVES

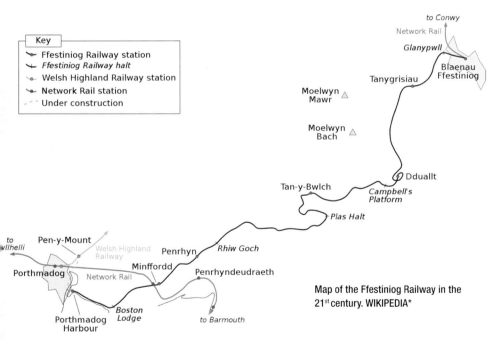

Map of the Ffestiniog Railway in the 21st century. WIKIPEDIA*

Preservation Society at the Great Northern Hotel at King's Cross in January 1953, and came on board.

Alan undertook a series of talks with the Ffestiniog company, leading to him and his nominees taking over control of the Festiniog board on June 24, 1954, following the handing over of a £2000 cheque. His shares were subsequently transferred to a charitable body in the form of the Ffestiniog Railway Trust. Led by an unpaid board of directors, enthusiastic volunteers backed by a small paid staff began rebuilding the line from Porthmadog to Blaenau Ffestiniog.

The restoration programme started on September 20, 1954, when Morris Jones, the foreman fitter who had last worked for the Festiniog in March 1947, rejoined the staff to complete the rebuilding of No. 2 *Prince* on which he had been engaged when Boston Lodge Works closed.

A special train to commemorate 60 years' service of line manager Robert Evans was run from Minffordd to Porthmadog on November 6, 1954.

Despite its legendary pioneering of narrow gauge steam, it was an internal combustion locomotive which hauled

the Festiniog's first heritage era passenger service. It ran from Porthmadog Harbour station across the Cob to Boston Lodge, behind *Mary Ann*, a 1917-built four-wheeled Motor-Rail Simplex First World War trench railways locomotive which the railway had bought in 1923. However, it was soon replaced by *Prince* which had by then been reassembled and returned to service on August 3, 1955.

The services were extended to Minffordd in 1956, Penrhyn in Easter 1957 and Tan-y-Bwlch in 1958.

However, black storm clouds loomed over the revival when plans by the British Electricity Authority for a hydroelectric power scheme near Tanygrisiau were unveiled in 1954. It involved the building of a huge reserrvor, Llyn Ystradau, which would flood part of the line including Moelwyn Tunnel – severing the restored section from the eastern terminus forever.

Despite loud protests, the compulsory purchase of the railway above Moelwyn Tunnel went ahead in 1956, but the revivalists vowed to continued their push to Blaenau, and in doing so they would prove that railway preservation was the art of the possible.

In 1962, a hugely-ambitious survey for a new route along the eastern side of the reservoir was carried out. It included a spiral loop at Dduallt, which would be unique on a public railway in Britain, and which would allowed the line to gain 35ft in height around and rejoin the old line at Tanygrisiau by running over the crest of the reservoir dam. On January 3, 1965, the first sod of what became known as the 'deviation' was turned.

As a first step in extending services eastwards, the line was reopened as far as Dduallt, the last station before the reservoir, in 1968. A new 310-yard tunnel through Moelwyn Mountain was built between 1975-1977 and full-length passenger trains first ran from Dduallt through the new tunnel to a temporary terminus known as Llyn Ystradau along-side the reservoir on June 25, 1977.

Tanygrisiau station reopened to traffic on June 24, 1978, and a new joint station with British Rail was built on the site of the town's GWR station, into which Ffestiniog trains first ran on May 25, 1982, marking the 150th anniversary of royal assent to the Festiniog Railway Act of 1832. The new joint station was officially opened on April 30, 1983 by George Thomas, Speaker of the House of Commons.

It then became clear that the extended line would need more motive power, and rather than restore another England saddle tank, such as *Welsh Pony*, it was decided to go for greater power in the form of a new double Fairlie, built at Boston Lodge Works, just as in pre-preservation days. In 1979, the new *Earl of Merioneth* emerged from the works, and was followed by a second

In the heritage era, Boston Lodge Works has built several new locomotives, the first being double Fairlie *Earl of Merioneth* in 1979. With the town's giant trademark slate waste heaps as a background, double Fairlie *Earl of Merioneth* steams out of Blaenau Ffestiniog station at the head of the 1.40pm to Porthmadog on September 19, 2009, with Western Region diesel hydraulic D1015 Western Champion at the head of Pathinder Tours 'Western Slater' main line outing from Didcot and its train stabled in the Conwy Valley Line run-round loop. ROGER DIMMICK/Ff&WHR

On July 4, 2007, double Fairlie *David Lloyd eorge*, which was built in 1992, heads a train marking the 175th anniversary of the Ffestiniog Railway. Ff&WHR ARCHIVES

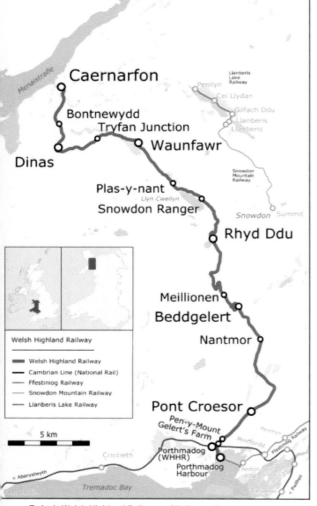

Today's Welsh Highland Railway, with the northern Caernarfon to Dinas section added to the route of the original. WIKIPEDIA*

double Fairlie, *David Lloyd George*, in 1992, and replica single Fairlie 0-4-0T *Taliesin* appeared in 1999. In 2010, the works turned out Lyd, which was

based on original Lynton & Barnstaple Railway Manning Wardle 2-6-2T *Lew*. The achievements of Boston Lodge Works in the heritage era are many, the latest at the time of writing being the above-mentioned return to steam of *Welsh Pony*.

SECOND TIME ROUND FOR THE WHR

As the nascent heritage sector began to gather pace, there were those who wondered if they could go one better than to revive a dormant but extant line – and rebuild one that had been closed and lifted – the Welsh Highland, perhaps?

A group of like-minded enthusiasts joined together to form the Welsh Highland Railway Society in 1961, with the seemingly very overambitious aim of doing just that. The society then turned itself into the Welsh Highland Light Railway (1964) Limited. This group was the precursor to what eventually became WHR Ltd.

Legal problems meant they were unable to take over the old company so, in the 1970s, the 1964 company purchased the former standard gauge exchange sidings (the Beddgelert Siding) near Tremadog Road in Porthmadog from British Rail and set up its Gelert's Farm base. In 1980, it began running passenger services over the mile-long line that is now known as

the Welsh Highland Heritage Railway, a separate organisation. The company also acquired original Welsh Highland locomotive *Russell*.

After the original line closed, *Russell* found a new home working at the Brymbo Ironworks railway in Oxfordshire, and then on Fayle's Tramway, a ball clay line on the Isle of Purbeck in Dorset. From there, it was saved by the Birmingham Locomotive Club for £50 and moved to the Talyllyn Railway for display. Sadly, the other survivor, *Moel Tryfan*, which had lain dismantled at Boston Lodge Works since 1934, was sold off for scrap… by none other than the early Festiniog revivalists who had no funds to restore it. It did not fit the Festiniog loading gauge and although such a move would be unthinkable today, the scrap value would provide much-needed funds.

In the mid-Eighties, several Festiniog employees became concerned about the impact of possible competition on their doorstep from a rebuilt Welsh Highland, so in 1987 the Festiniog company offered to buy the trackbed from the Receiver for £16,000 to block any such plans. When in 1989 the offer became public, there was a significant backlash.

The following year a change of directors at the Festiniog company brought a change of heart. What appeared to be a U-turn saw the unveiling of a new plan: the creation of a new heritage line firstly at the northern end of the Welsh Highland route, starting not from Dinas, but at first over the former standard gage trackbed from Caernarfon (the line closed under Beeching in 1964), and then the restoration of the rest, thereby creating a 40-mile 'steam highway' from Caernarfon to Blaenau Ffestiniog.

In 1993 the Ffestiniog launched its own Welsh Highland Railway Society as a focal point for volunteers interested in rebuilding the line. The 1964 company joined forces with Gwynedd County Council to oppose the Festiniog company's bid to take over the trackbed, but the Secretary of State was minded to grant the Welsh Highland Railway (Transfer) Light Railway Order on March 4, 1995, and on August 17 1999, the Official Receiver finally wound up the original Welsh Highland company.

A major boost to the Ffestiniog project came in 1995 when the Millennium Commission announced that it would give £4.3 million in funding to the Welsh Highland project to commemorate the year 2000. Further grants from the European Regional Development Fund, the Wales tourist board and the Welsh Development Agency were forthcoming and Gwynedd Council handed over the Caernarfon-Dinas trackbed to the railway on a 999-year lease for £1, in return for the cycleway that used the route being rebuilt.

The Caernarfon-Dinas section was officially opened on October 13, 2007. In the

November 25, 2018 saw legendary original Welsh Highland Railway flagship Russell returned to the route 81 years on when it completed a gauging and inspection run on November 25 from the Gelert's Farm base of its owner the Welsh Highland Heritage Railway over part of the 'main line' that it had not visited since 1937. The run was made possible owing to the close working relationship that has developed between its owner and the separate Ffestiniog & Welsh Highland Railways. Ff&WHR

If only the Welsh Highland Railway has motive power of this magnitude first time round! In 2011, reimported Manchester, 1958-built NGG16 articulated Beyer Garratt takes on water in readiness for its next trip up the line. ROBIN JONES

22 days that it ran that year, the short line carried 9200 passengers, evoking somewhat the optimism of the builders of the original Welsh Highland.

However, a Transport & Works Order was still needed by the Ffestiniog for the rebuilding of the original Welsh Highland Railway. Following a heated public inquiry, Deputy Prime Minister John Prescott announced on April 8, 1999 that he was minded to approve the Ffestiniog scheme.

The section from Dinas to Waunfawr opening in August 2000 and following a visit by Prince Charles, it was extended to Rhyd Ddu on August 18, 2003. In September 2004, the Ffestiniog announced that £5 million of funding had been made available by the Welsh Assembly and the EU. Backed by a public appeal, funds were now available to pay for the rest of the line to Porthmadog, including a new flat crossing over the Cambrian Coast Main Line, four tunnels, three large river bridges, and a tramway-style street section in Porthmadog, crossing the Britannia Bridge to join the Ffestiniog once again at Harbour station.

The two sections of the rebuilt line were finally joined on February 28, 2009.

Watched by Caernarfon MP Hywel Williams, a ceremony at Harbour station

in Porthmadog saw the leaders of the two volunteer tracklaying teams fix a golden bolt to a fishplate the complete the 26-mile through route from Caernarfon.

On one side of this last gap stood Ffestiniog double Fairlie *Merddin Emrys*, while on the other side was newly-restored South African Railways NGG16 Garratt No. 87.

Herein lies a story in itself. In the Colonel Stephens era, inadequate motive power was among the problems suffered by the Welsh Highland. Lessons learned, the rebuilt railway was intended to be operated by powerful locomotives capable of hauling 12 coaches on gradients of up to 1-in-40 and in such a way as to reduce long-term maintenance costs.

The Festiniog company turned its attention to South Africa, where several giant 2ft gauge NGG16 articulated Garratt 2-6-2-+2-6-2 locomotives, built in Manchester by Beyer Peacock, had been declared redundant from the Alfred County Railway. Two NGG16s, Nos 138 and 143, and two Funkey Bo-Bo diesels, later renamed *Castell Caernarfon* and *Vale of Ffestiniog*, were duly imported. Six more NGG16s and two NG15 2-8-0s were subsequently obtained, along with ex-Tasmanian Government Railways

K1, the world's first articulated Garratt, which was restored and entered service in autumn 2006. Dwarfing the Ffestiniog engines, they appear as if they are all but standard gauge locomotives on 2ft gauge tracks!

The official 'Aberglaslyn Pass Opening Train', for invited guests only, left Caernarfon at 10am on May 21, 2009. Services were extended from Hafod y Llyn to Pont Croesor in April 2010 and the final section of the line to Porthmadog opened in January 2011. A landmark was reached in July 2011 when ticket revenue from the rebuilt Welsh Highland Railway exceeded that of the Ffestiniog for the first time, strongly suggesting that in terms of tourism appeal, the short-lived original line was decades ahead of its time!

Today, the combined 40-mile system is run under the banner of the Ffestiniog & Welsh Highland Railways, with general manager Paul Lewin in charge of both – in that respect a modern-day counterpart to Stephens and Austen. That pair would undoubtedly have been proud to see the Ffestiniog & Welsh Highland renowned throughout the world of one of the world's finest narrow gauge systems and a shining credit to North Wales and the UK in general.

Chapter 14

Baldwin 4-6-0T No. 44720 of 1917 *Joan* with a carriage and rake of trucks at Stretton station on September 16, 1930. CSRM

Ashover Butts station as seen in official Clay Cross Company postcard of 1936. CSRM

ASHOVER LIGHT RAILWAY

Colonel Stephens built a mineral railway in the Peak District – and it was used to carry passengers to the Rainbow's End!

When George Stephenson, the 'Father of the Railways', surveyed the route for the North Midland Railway between Derby and Leeds in the 1830s, he saw the potential for the development of a colliery at Ashover near where the line passed.

Accordingly, in 1937 he formed George Stephenson & Company and at Clay Cross built a colliery and coke ovens which began operations in 1840. When he died in 1848, the company passed to his son Robert who, four years later, sold his shares in it. The firm became the Clay Cross Company, which at one time was the largest independent employer in the UK.

Developing its mining interests, in 1918 the company bought the Overton Estate at Fallgate in the Amber Valley to access the limestone, fluorite, barytes and gritstone deposits there for use in its Clay Cross ironworks.

To carry the limestone from the quarries, it was proposed to construct a four-mile standard gauge line from the Midland Railway at Stretton, with a 2ft gauge rope-worked mineral railway serving Alton colliery. Such a line would need to be built under statutory powers as a light railway, because the company did not own the land it was earmarked to cross. However, under light railway powers, the line would also be obliged to carry passengers.

It was said that the company chairman, General Thomas Jackson, met Colonel Stephens during wartime visits

Baldwin 4-6-0T *Joan* and its train at the Ashover Light Railway's opening ceremony at Ashover Butts station on April 6, 1925. CSRM

to North Wales, and his firm became the proposed railway's consulting engineers to the end.

The plan for a standard gauge line was authorised in 1919, but it was not built because the cost estimates were too high. The following year, Stephens successfully argued that costs could be cut if the line was built to 2ft gauge, following a longer (seven miles) route made easier by less difficult land contours.

Construction started in 1922 using direct labour from the Clay Cross Company after powers for an extension

One of two Ashover Light Railway coaches which moved to the Lincolnshire Coast Light Railway. It is seen in the train which marked that line's reopening in 2009 after moving from Humberston near Cleethorpes to the Skegness Water Leisure Park. DAVID ENEFER/LCLR

Baldwin 4-6-0T *Joan*, with legendary Ashover driver Harold Skinner on the footplate, at Clay Cross on September 13, 1930. CSRM

and change of gauge were obtained. It used surplus rail from the War Department Light Railways from where locomotives and stock – including 70 standard WD D bogie wagon – were also sourced.

The line started at Clay Cross Works, just above the northern portal of the main line Clay Cross Tunnel. The main terminus and headquarters was Clay Cross & Egstow within the works itself.

From here, the line swung northwards out of the town, then curved westwards through 180° to avoid going through Clay Cross town centre. Crossing Chesterfield Road, now the A61, a steel girder bridge spanning 45ft and 16ft high was needed, along with a half-mile long approach embankment. Indeed, the bridge and embankment were the only major pieces of engineering on the entire route between Clay Cross and the terminus at Ashover. Shortly after the opening of the railway, the Pirelli Tyre Company at Burton-on-Trent had a large advertisement painted on the bridge and it became known as 'The Pirelli Bridge'.

Four further stations named Chesterfield Road, Holmgate, Springfield and Clay Lane were erected within the town boundaries of Clay Cross, with the next station being at Stretton.

Stations were also built at Hurst Lane, Woolley, Dalebank, Milltown, Fallgate,

Salter Lane (for Ashover), and the western terminus, Ashover Butts.

Titled the Ashover Light Railway, it opened to goods traffic in 1924 and formally to passengers on April 7, 1925. More than 100 guests were invited to share in the celebrations and enjoy a ride over the new line. Two special trains ran covered with flags and bunting.

As secretary and general manager, Stephens brought in Captain May from the Festiniog and Welsh Highland railways, but he left in 1927 after disagreements with General Jackson. The colonel also recruited Edward 'Teddy' Skinner from the Selsey Tramway as foreman ganger, and he was joined by his sons Harold, who became an engine driver, and Maurice.

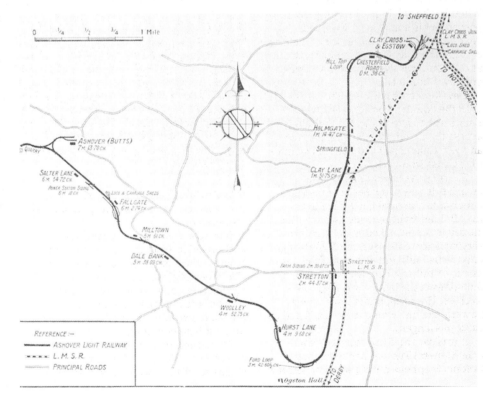

Sketch map of the Ashover Light Railway. THE RAILWAY MAGAZINE

An unidentified passenger train near Clay Cross in the mid-Twenties. CSRM

Baldwin 4-6-0T No. 44370 of 1936 *Hummy* near Stretton in August 1937. The locomotive last ran in 1946. CSRM

Clay Cross locomotive shed, with two unidentified locomotives in the background, and four loaded wagons in the foreground. CSRM

Baldwin 4-6-0T taking water at Fallgate on the last passenger train, on August 24, 1947. CSRM

mineral traffic, its passenger service proved successful during the mid-Twenties with eight daily services.

Summer services proved particularly popular with tourists lured by the scenery of the Amber Valley along which the line ran, and by 1927, three as opposed to the initial two passenger train sets were needed.

Capitalising on this public appeal, General Jackson had a wooden octagonal-shaped refreshment room built at The Butts, a level area at the Ashover terminus. He named it Where the Rainbow Ends after a popular children's play of the time. The building was easily recognisable as the roof was finished with multi-coloured tiles laid in the colours of the rainbow.

DEMISE AND CLOSURE

Such halcyon times were to be proved short lived. As on most other Stephens railways, competition from buses saw numbers decline and winter services ceased in October 1931.

All passenger services were withdrawn in September 1936, but the four large Gloucester Carriage & Wagon bogie carriages survived through the Second World War, and all ended up as stands on the Works bowling green. One was scrapped in 1960, but two were given a second life on the Lincolnshire Coast Light Railway, where they are numbered Nos. 1 and 2. No. 4 was moved to the Golden Valley Light Railway, the 2ft gauge line at the Midland Railway-Butterley.

The mineral traffic continued, but was hit hard by the closure of Milltown Quarry in 1936. The railway declined through the Second World War, with some locomotives cannibalised to keep the others going.

On September 9, 1946, General Jackson died aged 77. His son Humphrey took control of the Clay Cross Company but could not change the declining fortunes of the railway. Its last remaining contract with Butts Quarry was terminated in 1949.

The last steam locomotive worked on the line that same year, being superseded by a small Hibberd Planet 4w diesel mechanical locomotive that had been purchased new the year before, an which is now running on the Ffestiniog Railway as *Ashover*.

As he had done on the Welsh highland and Snailbeach District railways, Stephens again looked to ex-War Department Baldwin Class 10-12-D 4-6-0Ts to use both in the construction and operation of the line. The first four were named after General Jackson's children Peggy, Hummy (Humphrey), Joan and Guy. A fifth was named *Bridget*, and a sixth *Guy*, taking on the identity of the first *Guy* which was scraped as worn out in 1939.

Four passenger carriage bodies were bought from the Gloucester Carriage & Wagon Company for use on D wagon running gear, along with eight semi-open coach bodies from the 'Never Stop' narrow gauge railway at the 1925 British Empire Exhibition at Wembley.

In 1927, nearly 66,000 tons of mineral freight were carried, including much for onward shipment by the LMS. Although the line was built principally to carry

The society's restored Ruston 20 diesel. ALRS

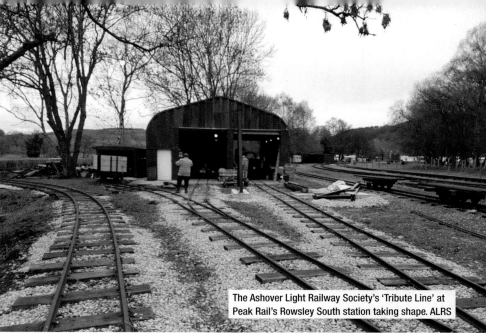

The Ashover Light Railway Society's 'Tribute Line' at Peak Rail's Rowsley South station taking shape. ALRS

The railway closed on March 31, 1950, shortly after Butts Quarry closed. The last train ran on October 23, 1950 when the Clay Cross Company's estate agent was conveyed in a wagon to survey the railway's land which could be sold. Scrap dealer Marple & Gillott, moved in the same day and began lifting of the track. In September 1951 the Pirelli Bridge was removed, marking the final stage in the dismantling of the railway.

However, a short length of track was left in place around the fluorspar plant at Milltown, and this section continued to operate until 1969, when it was replaced by road transport and lifted. It was worked by small diesel shunters and the surviving bogie wagons. The last surviving Ashover wagon may be a fluorspar quarry tub from Milltown Quarry now preserved at the Colonel Stephens Railway Museum at Tenterden Town on the Kent & East Sussex Railway (see Chapter 17).

REVIVAL IN TWO PLACES

The Ashover Light Railway Society was formed in 1996 with the aim of saving the surviving features of the railway. Members undertook a trackbed survey, and found that most of it between Ashover and Ogston Reservoir remained intact. Accordingly, the society modified its aim from preserving the line's remaining artefacts to reopening at least a short section.

One big problem is that after closure, the trackbed was sold to adjacent farmers in hundreds of sections, making the acquisition of a reasonable length with road access difficult.

In 2007, the society bought the Where the Rainbow Ends café, saving it from demolition. After the railway closed, it had been moved to John Street in Clay Cross. Supported by Ashover Parish Council, members dismantled it and placed it in secure storage for future re-erection, hopefully at Ashover Butts.

The society's main thrust though has always been to recreate the atmosphere of the old Ashover Light Railway, with the ultimate dream of seeing a Baldwin hauling ALR-style rolling stock.

In 2015, eager to start Ashover-like demonstration operations somewhere, the society began establishing a 2ft gauge running line at Peak Rail's Rowsley South headquarters. While no original Ashover locomotive survives, apart from the Hibberd Planet now on the Ffestiniog Railway, the society has acquired three locomotive for restoration.

Pride of its fleet is *Spondon*, is a 2ft gauge battery-electric vehicle built in 1926 by engineers of the Derbyshire and Nottinghamshire Electric Power Company for use in Spondon Power Station. The power station closed in 1972, and *Spondon* ended up at the now-closed Gloddfa Ganol Narrow Gauge Museum in Blaenau Ffestiniog.

It was acquired by the Ashover society in 2012 and restored at its engineering premises in Sheffield. In May 2017, the society accepted an invitation from the Ffestiniog Railway to run *Spondon* in its Quirks and Curiosities gala. It performed faultlessly, culminating in a solo run across the Cob into Porthmadog Harbour station.

The society had intended to begin operations in 2020 at Rowsley South site, adding another family attraction and extra dimension to standard gauge Peak Rail, but the plans were thwarted by the Covid-19 pandemic lockdown. At the time of writing, it was hoped to run the first society trains there in 2021 as an Ashover Light Railway 'Tribute Line', using its restored former Liverpool Corporation Water Works 1948-built Ruston & Hornsby 20DL diesel hauling a converted wagon with seats for up to six passengers.

Meanwhile, society officials continue to pursue their dream of acquiring a section of original Ashover trackbed and rebuilding it.

*Further details of the Ashover Light Railway Society may be obtained at www.alrs.org.uk

The Ashover Light Railway Society's restored unique battery electric locomotive *Spondon*. ALRS

An Edwardian hand-coloured postcard showing a tug at the entrance to the docks at Weston Point. ROBIN JONES COLLECTION

WESTON POINT LIGHT RAILWAY: THE COLONEL'S FORGOTTEN LINE

A million light years or more from the character of a 'typical' Colonel Stephens line, Cheshire's short Weston Point Light Railway was one of the last that he built, and is probably the most obscure.

Runcorn Docks in Cheshire date back to 1776 when the Bridgewater Canal opened at Runcorn. The town was at the western end of the canal which had a direct connection to the river Mersey via a set of locks. This link facilitated the onward movement of goods to Liverpool and a set of docks were built at the point where the river and the canal met.

A series of sidings were laid to serve the docks too, but these were not initially linked to the main line.

The Castner-Kellner Alkali Company opened a factory at the end of these sidings at Weston Point in 1897. The company was absorbed by Brunner Mond in 1920 before it and several other chemical companies merged to form Imperial Chemical Industries (ICI) in 1926. Salt Union at Weston Point also became part of ICI in 1940.

The London & North Western Railway agreed to build a single-track branch from Runcorn station on its Liverpool to Crewe line in 1920. The branch ran to a point known as Folly Lane, where it would fan out into the exchange sidings, which had to be upgraded to take an increased axle load.

Brunner Mond sought to build its own railway linking to this new branch. Known as the Weston Point Light Railway, it received its Light Railway Order on December 2, 1920, and the firm appointed Colonel Stephens as engineer.

This railway consisted of two fans of sidings divided by a level crossing at Sandy Lane. Other private lines linking it to the docks, quarries and chemical plans were also included in the new set-up. Brunner Mond (and later ICI) had its own locomotives for the system with a dedicated locomotive shed and repair facilities for both engines and wagons.

The line from Runcorn to Folly Lane is still in use today, as is the first fan of sidings on the Weston Point Light Railway as far as Sandy Lane.

Steam was replaced by diesel shunters in 1960 with ICI buying several Yorkshire Engine company 0-6-0 shunters. ICI operated an extensive tank wagon fleet and had around 300 twin axle wagons allocated to Folly Lane. In the late Eighties, ICI withdrew its own fleet of shunters, the last being donated to the Llangollen Railway for use on infrastructure trains. British Rail then assumed responsibility for shunting movements within the sidings and a Class 08 could often be seen.

To mark the 100th anniversary of ICI, the company hired GWR pannier tank No. 7754 from the Llangollen Railway as part of the celebrations to run on the branch.

A new £400 million energy-from-waste incinerator came into operator on the Weston Point Light Railway in 2014, with containers of compacted waste brought in by rail.

One of the largest energy recovery facilities currently operating in Europe, it converts pre-treated refuse-derived fuel produced from non-recyclable wastes into heat and energy. The facility generates up to 564 Gigawatt hours of electricity, enough to power the site itself and the equivalent of more than 150,000 homes, plus heat for exclusive use by the nearby chemical manufacturing site.

With the development of the power station and investment in the

Not exactly the locomotive you would expect to find at work on a Colonel Stephens light railway: English Welsh & Scottish Railway-liveried Class 66 diesel No. 66046 at Runcorn Folly Lane with a freight working to Arpley on March 4, 2011. FRED KERR

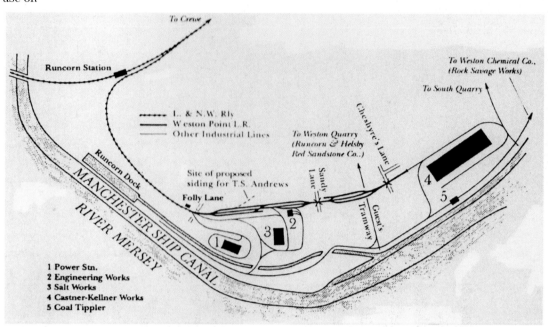

A plan of the Weston Point Light Railway and its place in the industrial system that serves Runcorn Docks. JOHN MILLER/CSRM

associated loading facilities, the future of the Folly Lane branch is looking bright again. It has gone from a rundown stretch of railway to a working branch once more.

In conjunction with the construction of the new power station, there have also been improvements made to the

The new energy recovery power station on the site of the former ICI Weston Workshops has given the line a renewed lease of life. VIRIDOR

Direct Rail Services Class 33 pair Nos. 33030 and 33025 on the docks branch with a Sellafield to Runcorn working on August 20, 2002. FRED KERR

permanent way with new track and points laid and a large unloading crane for the containers of household refuse installed.

No – the Weston Point Light Railway will never be a tourist magnet along the lines of the Kent & East Sussex Railway, but the sidings have also been visited in recent years by enthusiast railtours exploring sections of track where passenger trains normally do not run.

Chapter 16

Arthur Neal MP, the Parliamentary Secretary to the Ministry of Transport. with Colonel Stephens cutting the first sod of the North Devon & Cornwall Junction Light Railway at Hatherleigh in 1922. CSRM

Southern Railway E1/R 0-6-2T No. 2695 and carriage No. 361 at Torrington on May 24, 1935. The E1/Rs were designed for light passenger and freight duties and rebuilt from earlier London, Brighton & South Coast Railway E1 0-6-0Ts originally built 1874-1883. The rebuilt locomotives were intended to be used in the West of England. CSRM

NORTH DEVON & CORNWALL JUNCTION LIGHT RAILWAY:
THE LAST WORD

When British Railways closed what had been the North Devon & Cornwall Junction Light Railway from Torrington to Halwill Junction in 1965, there were many who wondered why this late-in-the-day Colonel Stephens line had ever been built.

Prior to the opening of the Channel Tunnel Rail Link, known today as High Speed 1, on November 14, 2007, the last trunk route of the age of railway building was the Great Central Railway's London Extension, from Annesley in Nottinghamshire, to Marylebone. The 92-mile route, designed for high-speed running throughout, opened for coal traffic on July 25, 1898, to passengers on March 15, 1899 and to goods on April 11, 1899.

In September 1905, the Great Western Railway began building its Last main

A disused area of the Meeth ball clay works has been turned into a nature reserve crossed by the Tarka Trail. TONY ATKIN*

line – its route from Birmingham to Cheltenham via Stratford-upon-Avon. The line opened to goods traffic on December 9, 1907, and to passengers on July 1, 1908.

However, the age of motor traffic had begun by then, and a new era was dawning fast. The national rail network had essentially expanded to its greatest extent and history would show that progressive shrinkage would be its next major phases, albeit several decades in the future.

However, a small additional piece joined the network jigsaw as late as 1925. Built by none other than Colonel Stephens, it was the last standard gauge public railway to be built before modern times.

Way back in 1865, the London & South Western Railway gave a parliamentary undertaking to extend the North Devon Railway from Bideford to Great Torrington. It tried to argue that the declining importance Great Torrington did not justify the expense of building a railway to serve it, but nonetheless the company was forced to comply with its obligations. It opened a new passenger station at Bideford, immediately east of the town bridge, on June 10, 1872, as the original terminus was unsuitable for use on the extension, and became the town's goods station. The line from Bideford to Torrington opened on July 18, 1872.

This new line was met by a 3ft gauge railway coming from the south the following year – the private Torrington & Marland Railway which was built to serve ball clay traffic from local pits. It was surveyed in 1879 by John Barraclough Fell, who was also the consulting engineer to Cornwall's Pentewan Railway. Fell designed the line with 10 patent wooden viaducts, an unusual but distinctive feature.

Part of the agreement with the landowners over whose land the line crossed was that it would carry local passengers as well as freight. Steam locomotives were used on both the Torrington & Marland main route and the internal lines in the pits.

Meanwhile, there was pressure to extend the standard gauge line to Plymouth, but again there was no money to be made from such a venture, and several schemes, including two empowered by Acts of Parliament in 1895 and 1901, came to nothing. It seemed that the only way forward to build a line serving what was a very sparsely-populated farming community was to build a light railway.

Enter the Colonel.

From 1905 onwards, Stephens drew up plans for a light railway from Torrington to Halwell Junction where it could meet the LSWR's Bude and North Cornwall lines while providing a cheap means of rural transport in an area otherwise disenfranchised from the network. Had

the line been built direct to Okehampton, rather than a junction in the middle of nowhere, it might well have encouraged more passenger use.

Stephens personally negotiated the finance to build the line.

An application for powers to build Stephens' line was made in 1909 and was

Hele bridge under construction with Colonel Stephens in 1924. CSRM

Map showing the North Devon & Cornwall Junction Light Railway and its connections

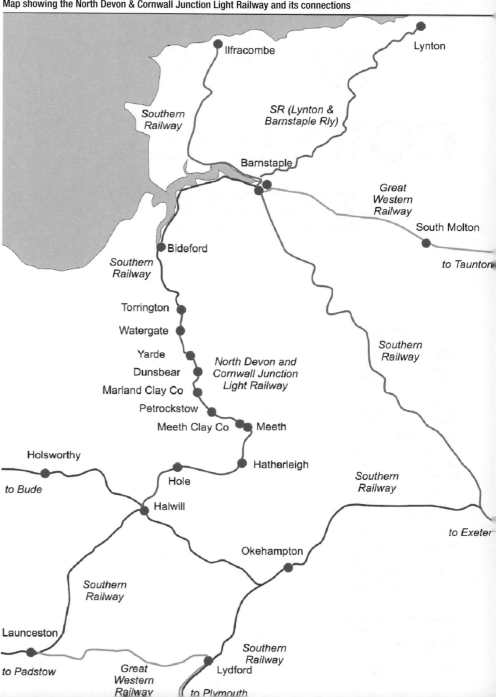

Ivatt 2MT 2-6-2T No.41216 about to depart Hatherleigh station. CSRM

Dunsbear Halt, pictured in June 1969, was the most used of all the halts on the North Devon & Cornwall Junction Light Railway because it was the closest to one of the ball clay works and generate commuter traffic from staff.

finally authorised in 1914, only for the First World War to halt proceedings.

The scheme was revived in 1919 but by then the cost of building the light railway had more than doubled. Stephens sought financial support from the government as well as local councils and for once received it, having successful argued the case that his railway would alleviate unemployment and hardship.

SLOW START TO PROTRACTED FAILURE

The first sod was cut in 1922 by an established contractor, who shipped in unemployed men to build the line. However, the workforce lacked both the necessary skills and the motivation to do the job. This, combined with poor weather, meant progress was painfully slow.

Unrest within the workforce led to a near-riot in June 1923 when a mob of up to 40 workers was held off by two policemen.

The contractor became bankrupt in 1925 and Stephens personally took over the construction of the final stages of the line.

Built as cheaply as possible and partly following the alignment of the 3ft gauge tramway, the railway had continuous sharp curves and ruling gradients in the range of 1-in-45 to 1-in-50.

Once completed, the light railway was opened without formality on July 27, 1925. It was operated by the Southern Railway as the successors to the LSWR.

Yet times had moved on and the ascendancy of motor traffic prevented the light railway from becoming a success. Hatherleigh, the main town on the line,

Ivatt 2MT No. 41312 awaits departure from Ropley at its Mid-Hants Railway home on June 29, 2019. Built at Crewe in May 1952, No. 41312 spent its entire working career on the Southern Region. First allocated to Faversham, it moved to Ashford in June 1959, before relocating to Barnstaple Junction where it worked over the Torrington branch. It famously performed the last steam service on the Lymington branch in April 1967. GARETH EVANS

Yarde Halt on the North Devon & Cornwall Junction Light Railway as seen in 1969. There were only a handful of houses near this intermediate stop.

Halwill Junction was the southern terminus of the North Devon & Cornwall Junction Light Railway. Southern Railway Maunsell N 2-6-0 No. 31845 heads through for Okehampton and Exeter on April 17, 1964. BEN BROOKSBANK*

The last public passenger train to Petrockstowe on the North Devon & Cornwall Junction Light Railway was a private enthusiasts' charter which ran on August 9, 1981. WILLIAM DAVIES

Meeth Hall now serves as a starting point for the Tarka Trail. DEREK HARPER*

Watergate Halt, now part of the Tarka Trail, was a remote rural stop with one small siding used by a local farmer. RON STRUTT*

lay only eight miles from the regional centre of Okehampton but more than 20 miles by rail. Also, passengers found the other stations inconvenient to use, being sited a considerable distance from the village they purported to serve.

The traffic from the clay works used it. Indeed, the building of the railway encouraged a new clay works at Meeth which, like the earlier venture at Marland, relied of effective transport. The Meeth (North Devon) Clay Company began operations in 1920 and laid a 2ft gauge line from its Woolladon works to the new line, and later worked pits nearer to the light railway. The narrow gauge line survived until 1970.

However, the hoped-for levels of agricultural traffic failed to materialise and it was largely the clay traffic and passenger services used by the clay companies' workers that kept the line alive.

Opened after the Grouping if 1923, there was no obligation for it to become part of a Big Four company and the Southern Railway refused to take it, although it operated it until nationalisation. Torrington was regarded as an end-on junction and at Halwill Junction, the light railway's trains were not even allowed into the main platforms.

With hindsight, it may seem remarkable that the line lasted into the Beeching era, having become part of British Railways at nationalisation on January 1, 1948.

Clay traffic apart, all freight facilities on the light railway were withdrawn on September , 1964 and the passenger service ended on March 1, 1965. round the same time the ne south of Meeth to Halwill nction, was completely osed and lifted.

Passenger services were axed from the Barnstaple-Torrington line just seven months later and the residents of Bideford found themselves disenfranchised from the national network.

The clay traffic on the route to the pits through Torrington continued for some years but never recovered fully after a rail drivers' strike in the 1970s. The clay companies began supplementing the line with road transport and were unwilling to invest in modern railway wagons.

Milk trains over the North Devon Railway line from Torrington to Bideford, Barnstaple and beyond stopped in 1978. They constituted the last milk train on the former Southern Railway/Region.

Ball clay trains and the occasional passenger special used the line until 1982, with total closure coming in 1983. There were several calls for it to be opened but these came to nothing.

The line was lifted and much of the trackbed now forms part of the Tarka Trail long-distance footpath and cycleway, which runs south as far as Meeth

The Lea Valley Railway Club's 'Atlantic Coast Express' excursion at Meeth clay quarry, on April 12, 1980. WILLIAM DAVIES

and north all the way to Bideford, Barnstaple and Braunton. Bideford station has become a railway museum with a short operation length of track.

TARKA VALLEY RAILWAY

After full closure, the Torrington station building was converted first into a public house and then to the Puffing Billy Restaurant and licensed café by owner Phil Simkin. British Rail had left some track in situ at the station, paving the way for the green shoots of a revival of sorts.

Wednesday, March 29, 2006, was to be a landmark day in the history of the station, for a genuine Southern Region Mk.1 TSO coach was delivered and placed back on the tracks.

No. S3924, built in 1954/5 at Eastleigh Carriage Works, arrived around midday from the now-closed Coventry Railway Centre on the back of one of the largest low-loaders to have ever visited Torrington. Having been routed along the M5 and then the A30 to Okehampton, and then on to the A386, the convoy became stuck in roadworks and had to take an even narrower route as a diversion.

On arriving at Torrington under escort, it first negotiated the main street causing some consternation and surprise to passing motorists and onlookers alike. And as if by magic, at just after midday, to the sound of air-horns blasting around the corner and over the bridge appeared the low-loader with its valuable cargo.

At the station, the low-loader reversed into position alongside the platform edge and up to the ramp erected earlier that morning. Slowly the carriage was winched down the railed ramp and on to the existing track to take up its position alongside the newly-resurfaced Up platform.

A champagne reception and buffet was laid on for the many invited guests who by now had assembled to witness this historic event, including the Mayor of Torrington, Coun Richard Rumbold. One of his predecessors, Coun Clifford Quick, had waved off the last revenue-earning train in 1982. The guest of honour was Taffy Lonergan, the last surviving member of the station staff, who recalled many of the happy years he had spent there.

A fully-fledged revivalist group, the Tarka Valley Railway was set up in 2008. After a few years the group was reformed into a Charitable Incorporated Organisation with the objectives of "preserving for the public benefit and to maintain the Tarka Valley Railway line through the Torridge Valley and to advance education about the history of transportation in the Torridge Valley area, and railways in particular".

The overall plan sees the railway extended back to Bideford alongside the

Tarka Trail footpath/cycleway. Phase 1 involves development over a period of time covering construction of, and settling in of, the first phase of the operation which will take the railway as far as the first overbridge (Bridge 136), but in the Bideford direction.

Preparation for the next phases will be ongoing and each phase will build on the existing phases, reviewed in the light of experience, available finance and any changes in the prevailing economic and social environment, plus the support of local and county authorities and government.

A pedestrian/cycle crossing at the end of the platform and an emergency vehicle crossing have already been installed.

An appeal in 2020 helped to fund the purchase a point leading to the station's kick-back siding and this has been delivered to site. Once it is in place, three 60ft railway track panels and a buffer stop will then be installed, taking the main line as far as the first bridge in the Bideford direction.

The necessary staff training will be carried out and the railway will then be in a position to offer 'brake van' rides to

Members of the Torrington Cavaliers English Civil War re-enactment group cross swords next to the diesel shunter named after the group. PHIL TARRY/TVR

John Fowler 0-4-0 diesel No. 4000001 of 1945 on the new pedestrian crossing at Torrington in November 2019. TVR

Torrington station today viewed from the road overbridge looking towards Bideford with the Puffing Billy on the right. TVR

the public thus becoming an operational heritage railway.

As the railway develops, work will be carried out to set up a heritage centre for the display and dissemination of information regarding the history and development of transport in the Torridge area, in particular that relating to railways. Provision for educational visits and talks will be made.

*Donations are needed to ensure completion of this early but pivotal part of the heritage railway's long-term plan to expand to Bideford. Contributions may be sent either by cheque made payable to Tarka Valley Railway at Torrington Station, Torrington, Devon EX38 8JD, or by internet to Barclays Bank, sort code 20-04-59, Account no 33321045 quoting 'Point appeal'. Email tarkavalleyrailway@gmail.com for more details or to arrange a visit.

NEW DIESEL TORRINGTON

A large crowd gathered at Torrington station (aka the Puffing Billy pub and restaurant complex) on Saturday, August 19, 2017, to see the Tarka Valley Railway's new locomotive officially named *Torrington Cavalier*.

After an introduction by railway chairman Mark Smith, the unveiling of the nameplate was carried out by Mark Keeley, chairman of re-enactment group the Torrington Cavaliers, after which a bottle of champagne was broken on the running plate of the Ruston Hornby locomotive.

Many of the Cavaliers were present in full regalia and the occasion was supported by the mayor of Torrington, several past mayors, local, district and county councillors, officials from Rotary, the Balsdon Trust and other

Fowler 0-4-0 diesel shunter *Peter*, which was built in 1940 for the North Devon Clay Company at Meeth to work the company's extensive network connecting its clay trains to the North Devon & Cornwall Junction Light Railway, in mid-2017 ran for the first time since 1962 in 2017. At the end of its working life it was acquired by a group of Bodmin & Wenford Railway volunteers with a view to preservation, and a full restoration programme began in 2014. BWR

local dignitaries. Afterwards, the invited guests adjourned to the Puffing Billy for a buffet lunch.

The six-cylinder 192hp diesel shunter was the last of its type to be built, in February 1969.

It was supplied new to the Nevils Dock & Railway company in Llanelli and worked there until 1990. It was preserved at the Chasewater Railway from where it was acquired by the Torrington revivalists of the LSWR line.

END OF ANOTHER ERA

Clay extraction at the Meeth pits stopped in 2004, bringing a 127-year industrial history to a close.

Owner Imerys undertook a restoration programme of the 370-acre site, which

includes two major former quarries which have now been flooded to form lakes.

In early 2013, Imerys sold the former Meeth clay works to the Devon Wildlife Trust to develop it as a nature reserve. It was marketed at an asking price of offers in excess of £550,000 and sold for an undisclosed sum.

Harry Barton, chief executive of Devon Wildlife Trust added: "I am absolutely thrilled that we are in a position to take on this exciting site.

"This is largely thanks to support from Viridor Credits Environmental Company and generous individual donors. We will be working hard to develop the site as a nature reserve."

Chapter 17

A waxwork of Colonel Holman F Stephens in a replica of his Tonbridge office stuffed with original documents and artefacts. ROBIN JONES

THE KING'S
TREASURE TROVE

Curator Brian Janes describes the award-winning Colonel Stephens Railway Museum at Tenterden Town station on the Kent & East Sussex Railway.

It was 25 years ago that a group of enthusiasts started work on adapting a run down Second World War corrugated iron hut to produce an award-winning museum that enhances any visit to the Kent & East Sussex Railway. Today it entertains around 16,000 visitors every year.

Although the railway was revived as a living example of an independent branch line, interest in its founder, engineer and manager Holman Fred Stephens became increasingly apparent.

Stephens is one of those larger-than-life characters who have grabbed the

imagination of enthusiasts perhaps only, and unfairly, for the sturdy independence of their latter years. Interest has broadened out to encompass all the railways he built, promoted or ran in his very active life.

From the late Victorian era till the First World War, light railways were thought of as a method of bringing transport to rural areas, cheaply built for later improvement. Stephens and others sought to bring this vision to fruition with their engineering and management skills. He became the leading independent

engineering dynamic behind the light railway movement, recognised in the highest circles of government, and so brought much needed transport to some deprived rural areas. From 1920 fierce motor transport competition and the Grouping of most railways changed the direction of Stephens' business and he became less a promoter and builder and more a valued manager of the remaining independent railways.

Stephens was of course a man of his time and, like the 1896 Light Railways Act so associated with him, was perhaps

Taking pride of place inside the museum is Shropshire & Montgomeryshire 0-4-2 well tank No. 1 *Gazelle*, which is owned by the National Railway Museum. What is said to be the smallest standard gauge locomotive in Britain was built as a 2-2-2WT in 1893 by Alfred Dodman & Co at King's Lynn to a design produced by S Stone of the Great Eastern Railway. It was rebuilt as 0-4-2WT in 1911 by W G Bagnall Ltd when it also gained an enclosed cab.

After withdrawal, *Gazelle* was preserved and sent to the Transportation Centre of the Royal Engineers at Longmoor in Hampshire in 1950 where it was placed on display on the edge of the parade ground. When the Longmoor Military Railway closed in 1970, *Gazelle* was reclaimed by the Science Museum and was displayed at York Railway Museum for the next 25 years and the Museum of Army Transport at Beverley. In 1997 *Gazelle* moved to Tenterden where it was placed on display.
ROBIN JONES

born too late. Although the observably crumbling elements of his achievements regrettably became all that was evident to later, and indeed current, generations, nevertheless his energy and the achievements of his heyday were notable, and acknowledged as such.

It is this story that the museum sets out to illustrate and celebrate.

The core of the rich collection of artefacts was established in the 1960s largely through the foresight of Philip Shaw, a prominent early and continuing leading member of the revived Kent & East Sussex Railway, who began setting aside items donated by former employees of the Stephens empire. William Austen junior, the son of Stephens' principal assistant and successor, in particular, was a considerable source of material.

At the closure at nationalisation of Colonel Stephens' office at Salford Terrace, Tonbridge, a large chest and Stephens' roll top desk were stuffed with papers and small artefacts relating to the various companies and this sat unopened for 30 years or so in the porch of Austen's home. It proved to be a veritable treasure trove, which has taken many years to be sorted, displayed and indexed. We must be thankful that other employees who venerated Stephens and his work also retained material from their offices, since although a little did pass to the British Railways archives, the bulk was taken away and burned.

The surviving chassis from the first coach built for the Rye & Camber Tramway is displayed outside the museum. It was last used after the line closed in 1939, for transporting navy personnel to Rye Harbour in the run-up to D-Day. It was sold after the war for use as a chicken coop. It was rescued by enthusiasts in the mid-Sixties, but the wooden body had rotted too much to be saved. ROBIN JONES

With the notable exception of the Ffestiniog Railway (the records for which are currently cared for elsewhere), many of the papers and artefacts relating to Stephens' railways which went to the wall or were not nationalised were, if not destroyed, rescued by enthusiasts and survived in private hands. Thanks to their subsequent generosity and purchases with the museum's modest funds this material is slowly and painstakingly being reassembled to produce a rounded picture of the man and his railways.

Stephens' father was a founder member of the pre-Raphaelite Brotherhood school of painters and the first exhibits presented to the viewer celebrate his boyhood and subsequent private life as a bachelor. These range from his first toy train to his Masonic regalia, vesta case, and his cigar case with his last unsmoked cigar left on his death in the Admiralty Hotel at Dover. A particular prize in the archive is the collection of family letters and papers spanning nearly 50 years.

One of the centrepieces of the museum that comes from the Austen hoard is a replica of the colonel's office in Tonbridge, containing all of the furniture and paraphernalia. This includes his roll-top desk and office chair, wicker filing trays, ledgers, pictures, rubber stamps, brief case and even pens, pencils and pieces of chalk. We also have the colonel's drawing office and surveying equipment.

Although his interests and associates were wide Stephens' sole hobby seems to have been his voluntary engineering military activities, commemorated in an exhibit, which lead eventually to his colonelcy. However he also seems to have had a penchant for railway passes, only some of which he used and was particularly proud of. On display is most of his collection of 72 wallet or card and watch chain passes, mostly from the immediate pre-grouping years of 1921/1922, usually first class and including many minor companies. We have a second collection of free passes all issued to W H Austen, many of which are second or third class perhaps indicating his role as Stephens' long time junior assistant.

The collection embraces material from all the 16 railways associated with Colonel Stephens and a general selection of artefacts may be seen in the museum. Included are timetable posters, trespass signs, nameplates, permanent

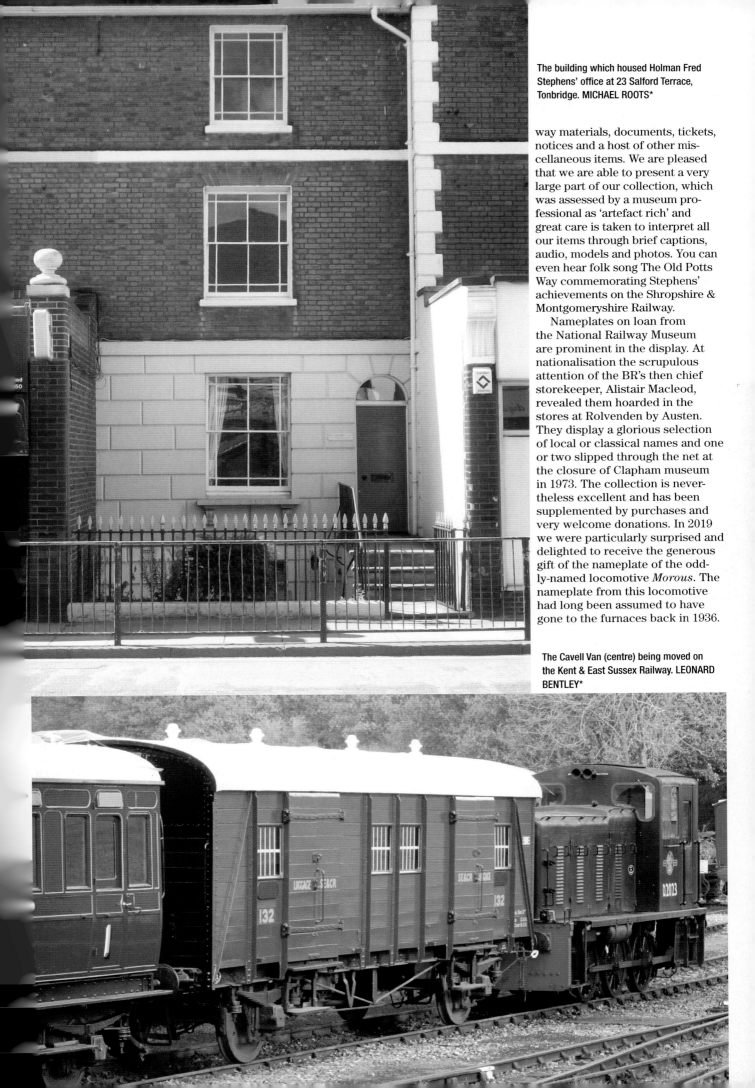

way materials, documents, tickets, notices and a host of other miscellaneous items. We are pleased that we are able to present a very large part of our collection, which was assessed by a museum professional as 'artefact rich' and great care is taken to interpret all our items through brief captions, audio, models and photos. You can even hear folk song The Old Potts Way commemorating Stephens' achievements on the Shropshire & Montgomeryshire Railway.

Nameplates on loan from the National Railway Museum are prominent in the display. At nationalisation the scrupulous attention of the BR's then chief storekeeper, Alistair Macleod, revealed them hoarded in the stores at Rolvenden by Austen. They display a glorious selection of local or classical names and one or two slipped through the net at the closure of Clapham museum in 1973. The collection is nevertheless excellent and has been supplemented by purchases and very welcome donations. In 2019 we were particularly surprised and delighted to receive the generous gift of the nameplate of the oddly-named locomotive Morous. The nameplate from this locomotive had long been assumed to have gone to the furnaces back in 1936.

The interior of the restored Cavell Van. HUGH NIGHTINGALE*

researchers of Stephens and his lines.

We receive many requests for copies of photographs but quite frankly we just do not have the voluntary resources to provide such a service. We co-operate with a limited number of established authors and the Colonel Stephens Society, and photographs acknowledged to 'Colonel Stephens Railway Archive' come from the Tenterden archives. Although usually not individually credited, many other illustrations of handbills, tickets or correspondence are also from our collection.

The beginnings of the collection were first drawn together by the late John Miller, the founding curator, and displayed in 1977 in the Town Museum in Station Road, Tenterden in what was once the railway stables owned by Holman Stephens personally.

From 1995 the use of the building in premises adjacent to the station at Tenterden proved a massive step forward organised by John. The building itself is a wartime structure, a type of large Nissen type building called a Romney hut, probably used in 1943 for components for Operation PLUTO before use as a food store. The hugely enlarged area enabled the presentation and interpretation we now provide. However, we have probably reached the limits of what can be achieved in our 'quart in a pint pot'.

Indeed, we now have interesting outdoor exhibits like the tramcar chaise from the 3ft gauge Rye & Camber tram and, under its dedicated shelter, a replica of Stephens' famous Ford railmotor featured in the recent book Colonel Stephens and his Railmotors authored by museum volunteers using its records and photographs

The present display is designed to inform and entertain a general non-specialist visitor through displays, models and film for an hour. For many years we had charged a small fee but for the last few years it has been free with the opportunity to make donations. This has increased visitor numbers although we are some way from breaking even and still subsidise the museum both with our volunteering and cash raising efforts.

By some miracle it was acquired from the scrapman by a passing cyclist who, after a small financial transaction, rode away with the nameplate tied to his crossbar.

Perhaps the climax of the display is a locomotive part of the National Collection and, arguably, the smallest standard gauge locomotive in Britain, the Shropshire &Montgomeryshire locomotive *Gazelle*.

Hidden behind the public display is the archive research section, the historical papers dating from about the 19th century and which occupy many steel cabinet filing drawers and shelves. The photographic archive is considerable, though seldom are we given original negatives. Now indexed, there are at least 7000 photographs, the earliest of which were in the colonel's collection. The archive is open, by appointment, for

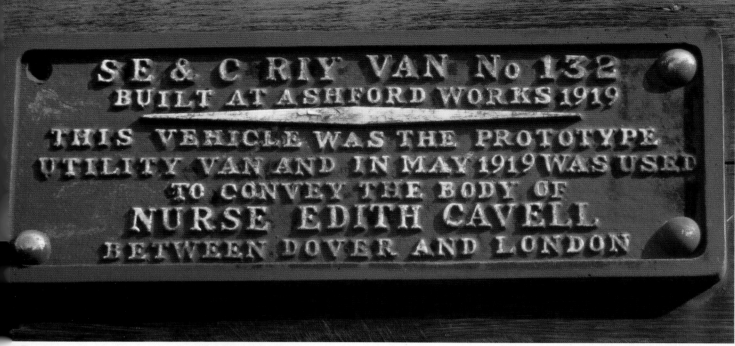

The plaque carried on the side of the Cavell Van. MICHAEL ROOTS*

We make a little go a long way but even so, without the occasional private donation we could not achieve as much as we do.

* The Mortons Media (*Heritage Railway* magazine) Interpretation Award for 2014 cited the museum's "continuing magnificent highlighting of a unique dimension of British railway history".

THE CAVELL VAN

The Colonel Stephens Railway Museum is also the custodian of the Cavell Van.

Designed by Richard Maunsell, it is the prototype four-wheeled Parcels and Miscellaneous Van (PMW) built by the South Eastern & Chatham Railway at Ashford Works in 1919 and numbered 132. That year, it was used to bring back the body of British nurse Edith Cavell from Belgium where she had helped 200 prisoners of war escape from the Germans before she was caught and murdered. Her body was bought back to England on a destroyer and transported by train from Dover to London. A service was held at Westminster Abbey before she was buried at Norwich Cathedral.

Two months later, it was used to carry the body of merchant mariner Captain Charles Fryatt, who was also shot by the Germans after being captured, and in November 1920 that of the Unknown Warrior, a soldier who had been killed on the Western Front, prior to the funeral service in Westminster Abbey on November 11, 1920.

The van passed to the Southern Railway in 1923 and was renumbered 972, then 374S on transfer to departmental service in August 1946. It was

used as a stores van serving Lancing Carriage Works and Brighton Works. Under British Railways it was numbered DS734 and was transferred to the internal user pool in October 1967 and renumbered 082757. The van ended its service at Guildford cable depot and was withdrawn from service in 1991 and stored at Hoo Junction.

It was sold to the Tenterden Rolling Stock Group in 1992 and moved to the Kent & East Sussex Railway being delivered to Wittersham Road in January 1992.

From 1994-2004 is was stored at Robertsbridge on the Rother Valley Railway before being returned to the Kent & East Sussex Railway in 2004. In December 2009, an appeal for £35,000 to fully restore the van was launched, a project which was completed as intended on November 10, 2010, the 90th anniversary of the carriage of the body of The Unknown Warrior. It is now used as a museum to commemorate The Unknown Warrior, Cavell and Fryatt and has visited other heritage venues.

In October 2015, the van was transported by road to Norwich as part of the commemorations for the 100th anniversary of Cavell's death.

THE COLONEL STEPHENS SOCIETY

Founded in 1985, the Colonel Stephens Society caters for followers of the light railways engineered or managed by Holman Fred Stephens, and has more than 300 members worldwide.

It produces a quarterly newsletter, The Colonel, covering news of the surviving

lines, historical articles, model-making and scale drawings.

Its now traditional members' weekend is held each May, when the society visits a railway with a strong connection with Stephens. It has a constitutional commitment to "encourage the preservation of any surviving relics of the railways engineered or managed by the colonel". As such, each year it makes donations to heritage projects, such as the restoration of locomotives and buildings with a Stephens connection.

In 2005, it gave £250 to the Colonel Stephens Railway Museum for the creation of the aforementioned waxwork, and in 2012 £1000 for its purchase of a works plate for the Kent & East Sussex Railway locomotive No.2 *Northiam*.

It has also given several hundred pounds to what is now known as the Welsh Highland Heritage Railway for the restoration of the line's flagship Hunslet 2-6-T *Russell*. It has also made grants to cover the overhauls of 'Terrier' tanks and many, many more projects.

In 2020, after the entire UK heritage sector ground to a halt in late March because of the Government lockdown regulations following the COVID-19 pandemic, the society gave funds to the museum and four of the colonel's lines – the Ffestiniog & Welsh Highland Railway, the Kent & East Sussex Railway, the Welsh Highland Heritage Railway and East Kent Railway to offset the impact of not having income from running trains to cover day-to-day running costs.

A full list of recipients of the numerous grants from the society – plus details of how to join – can be found at www. colonelstephenssociety.co.uk

The world's first standard gauge public passenger train on a heritage line: Hunslet 0-6-0DM is seen pushing Swansea & Mumbles Railway tramcar No. 2 during the inaugural week of volunteer-run Middleton Railway operations in June, 1960. MIDDLETON RAILWAY TRUST

The first train on the world's first public railway built by enthusiasts on a green field site: August 27, 1960 saw Simplex *Paul* (Motor Rail Simplex 4wDM No. 1926 of 3995 *Paul*) and a single War Department Class D wagon from the First World War trench railways used as an open passenger coach comprise the inaugural train on the 2ft gauge line at Humberston. BILL WOOLHOUSE COLLECTION/LCLR

THE SECOND AND BIGGEST LIGHT RAILWAY EMPIRE

Today's flourishing heritage railway sector is a sizeable plank of the UK tourist economy, and in so many respects, Colonel Stephens' portfolio of lines may be viewed as its predecessor.

The preceding chapters have detailed the light railways which were engineered by Colonel Stephens. However, as might be expected from a career workaholic engineer, the colonel was also involved in many other projects that did not bear fruit. Eighteen of them reached the Light Railway Order stage.

One early scheme that was never built was the Gower Light Railway, which was intended to serve coal villages in the Clyddach valley near Swansea, and on which Stephens worked in 1896.

The Gower, a designated Area of Outstanding Natural Beauty, already had a unique place in world railway history. It was on its eastern side that the Swansea and Mumbles Railway, which had opened in 1804 to serve limestone quarries, carried the world's first fare-paying railway passengers under an agreement effective from March 25, 1807.

While Stephens was living at Cranbrook he became friends with Edward Peterson, the son of the rector of Biddenden, the Rev William Peterson,

and a solicitor with a practice in Staplehurst. Before the Light Railways Act 1896 was passed, Edward Peterson developed an interest in the subject and claimed to have clients around the UK who were prepared to invest in such schemes.

Prior to the passing of the Act, in July 1895 Stephens and Peterson formed the Light Railways Syndicate, a company with the purpose of obtaining orders for new light railways. The pair's intention was that once the necessary powers had been granted to the Syndicate, a separate company would be set up to independently raise capital and build the railway.

It was claimed that the 12-mile Gower route could access 28 million tons of coal while providing a passenger service for 6000 local residents, and had the potential to turn Port Eynon into a holiday resort.

The scheme was approved in 1897, but around the same time separate proposals for a second railway route on Gower emerged, to run from Mumbles to

Rhossili along the south coast of the peninsula. Its goal would be to turn Rhossilli into a Brighton-style health resort for South Wales. It too was approved, but the slow progress on both was killed off by the outbreak of the First World War, and neither scheme was revived.

The Peterson Syndicate's next schemes, also involving Stephens, were the Hadlow (Kent) Light Railway, the Central Essex Light Railway, which would have linked Ongar with Dunmow, the Kelvedon, Coggeshall & Halstead and the St Just, Land's End & Great Western Junction, which had it been built, would have extended the UK railway network to a new western extremity at the far tip of Cornwall, rather than leaving it to stop at Penzance. None of these railways were ever built, due to an inability to raise the necessary capital, but the Syndicate did have one success, the Sheppey Light Railway, as described in Chapter 5.

The Syndicate was wound up in 1912 two years after Peterson went bankrupt Indeed, there had for long been grave

Sixty years to the day, Hunslet 0-6-0DM No. 1697 of 1932 as LMS No. 7501 heads the Middleton Railway 60th anniversary train past GN Curve on June 20, 2020. This time there was no tramcar, as it had been scrapped in 1969, and the train had to be run privately by the line's officials because the railway was closed to the public because of the Covid-19 lockdown. MIDDLETON RAILWAY

doubts as to whether sufficient investors would have been prepared to finance the Syndicate's scheme.

Another Stephens non-starter was the Southern Heights Light Railway, an electrified line from Orpington in Kent to Sanderstead in Surrey, which was authorised in 1925 and which was to have been operated by the Southern Railway. The scheme was abandoned in the 1930s.

Also after the First World War, a Worcester and Broom Light Railway was proposed, effectively extending the Stratford & Midland Junction Railway (see Chapter 11), with Stephens as its engineer. Before the Grouping of 1923, it might have made some economic sense, but in the age of the 'Big Four' companies, not so.

Stephens was also involved in plans to extend Shropshire Railways (reborn as the Shropshire & Montgomeryshire Light Railway) to Market Drayton, and further extensions to the East Kent Light Railways, that likewise did not come to pass.

Other 'damp squibs' included the East Sussex Railway, the Headcorn & Faversham Junction Railway, the Headcorn & Maidstone Junction Railway (the latter pair both effectively adding to the Kent & East Sussex Railway), the Hedingham & Long Melford Railway, the Long Melford & Hadleigh Railway, the Maidstone & Faversham Junction Railway, the Maidstone & Sittingbourne Railway, the Newport & Four Ashes Railway, the Orpington, Cudham & Tatsfield Railway and the Surrey & Sussex Railway.

Again, we have to look at the primary reason for the failure of these schemes, and for the demise of most of those that the colonel did build.

We had a superb, competent, imaginative and tireless engineer who had the vision and acumen to take railways where none had, for whatever reason, gone before. Had many of the abovementioned failed schemes been proposed 20 years earlier, it may well have been that they would have succeeded. Yet Stephens appeared at the end of the great railway building age, at the same time that the first cars were taking to the streets.

Maybe Stephens and his investors did not see the tidal wave that was motor transport about to engulf both them and their light railways, especially after the First World War. In many ways, no matter how ingenious his lines might have been, the writing was on the wall

The first former part of the British Railways network to be reopened as a heritage line under the provisions of the 1896 Light Railways Act: LBSCR A1X 'Terrier' 0-6-0T No. 55 Stepney leaves the crowded platforms at Sheffield Park with the first public Bluebell Railway passenger train on August 7, 1960. BLUEBELL RAILWAY ARCHIVE

Colonel Stephens survivor: as we saw it Chapter 10, 1885-built LSWR 0415 class Adams radial 4-4-2T No. 488 was part of the East Kent Light Railways fleet for several years in between main line service, and is now part of the Bluebell Railway fleet. ROBIN JONES

for them and in time for so much of the national rail network too; less commercially successful lines widely succumbed to cheaper and more versatile road transport, as illustrated never more forcefully than during the Beeching years of the Sixties.

Indeed, in terms of providing rail transport for the disenfranchised masses in rural areas, the 1896 Light Railways Act may be viewed as too little too late. In 1898 there were 88 applications for Light Railway Orders, but by 1914 that number had fallen to just two. However, the colonel, the acknowledged leader in the light railway sector, persevered with the concept after the end of the First World War, firmly believing that his budget-price local lines strategies and management style could still succeed against the tide of the national trend, by tackling individual and often unique local transport needs with bespoke affordable solutions.

RAILWAYS FOR RAILWAYS' SAKE

Colonel Stephens died on October 23, 1931, leaving his assistant William Austen to handle most of his railways' affairs. Yet just before then, what may have been the stirrings of a new breed of light railway empire, one which he could not have foreseen, had been on the cusp of bringing forth green shoots.

In April 1929, railway engineer Ron Shepherd tried to save Suffolk's 3ft gauge Southwold Railway which closed that year. He formed a consortium of local landowners, businessmen and town councillors and proposed raising money to buy the line through a bonds issue.

Had he succeeded, the 8½-mile Southwold Railway might well have become the world's first 'preserved' line, not only continuing to serve local public transport needs but also providing an attraction for the resort's summer visitors. Sadly the owning company refused to sell, and the line's locomotives and stock were finally scrapped for the war effort in 1942.

Indeed, the idea of running railways purely for pleasure or tourism purposes pre-dated Colonel Stephens. Sir Arthur Heywood built a 15in gauge miniature line on his Duffield Bank estate in Derbyshire in 1874, with the idea of selling it to a wider audience and in 1895 he built a similar one at Eaton Hall for the Duke of Westminster.

Wenman Joseph Bassett-Lowke, the most famous modelmaker of the early 20th century, and miniature locomotive engineer Henry Greenly formed a company called Miniature Railways of Great Britain in 1904 to develop such lines. Accordingly, the derelict 3ft gauge Ravenglass & Eskdale Railway in the Lake District, which had been opened in 1875 to transport hematite iron ore from mines near the village of Boot and soon afterward upgraded to carry passengers, was converted to 15in gauge and was operated by miniature steam locomotives in 1915. The 2ft gauge Fairbourne Railway south of Barmouth in mid-Wales, which opened in 1895 as a horse-drawn construction tramway, was also converted by the firm to 15in gauge in 1916.

However, these converted lines could not – at the start – be described as 'preserved' or 'heritage' lines, because the locomotives that ran on them were newly-built scale replicas of contemporary main line types, and were run as profitmaking tourist businesses without a thought of saving historical artefacts for future generations.

Was the colonel aware of the rescue attempt which accompanied the closure of the Southwold Railway? The story of railway 'preservation', that is, the saving of a line by volunteer effort, may well have had its beginnings in a letter from Manchester reader Arthur E Rimmer in the January 1941 edition of *The Modern*

The Lincolnshire Coast Light Railway's flagship locomotive, Peckett 0-6-0ST No. 1008 of 1903 *Jurassic*, was delivered new to the quarries and cement works of Kaye and Company in Southam in Warwickshire, from where it was acquired in 1961 after its final day in operation there. It is seen heading a train comprising the former Sand Hutton Railway coach and the line's two blue-liveried coached from Colonel Stephens' Ashover Light Railway. BILL WOOLHOUSE COLLECTION/LCLR

Tramway, the journal of the Light Railway Transport League.

He asked if the moribund Welsh Highland Railway passenger service, which had last run on September 5, 1936, could be reintroduced in order to save petrol supplies during the Second World War, possibly by railway enthusiast societies supplying free labour. Here was the first documented occasion that such a suggestion had been made, and fellow enthusiast Owen Prosser later credited the letter as the inspiration for his idea of forming a society to save the Talyllyn Railway.

Owen Prosser wrote to Minister of Transport JTC (later Lord) Moore-Brabazon in support of the Welsh Highland. The minister pointed out that the line, once part of the colonel's portfolio, had run at a loss since its opening in 1923, and that the track had been subsequently lifted.

However, on September 2, 1949, an anonymous letter appeared in *The Birmingham Post*, headlined 'Breakdown on Talyllyn Railway'.

The writer said that Fletcher Jennings 0-4-0WT No. 2 *Dolgoch*, by then the 2ft 3in gauge line's sole operative locomotive, had suffered a fractured frame and had to be withdrawn from service, leading to the two-days-a-week passenger service being suspended.

A reply in the newspaper's letters column came on September 9 from renowned transport author and waterways campaigner Tom Rolt. He congratulated the writer, but disagreed with his demand that either the Government or British Railways should step in to save the Talyllyn from closure.

Owen wrote to Tom and said that the best means of saving the Talyllyn would be a voluntary society, supplying both cash and free labour. The line had in 1910 been bought by local landowner and Liberal MP for Merioneth Henry Haydn Jones in 1910. He had died on July 2, 1950, after which the closure of the little line seemed inevitable.

However, Tom swung into history-making action, and called a public meeting on October 11 at the Imperial Hotel in Birmingham to consider the Talyllyn's future, with 36 well-wishers turning up. They elected a committee which met for the first time on October 23 when Owen's suggestion of the name for the new body, the Talyllyn Railway Preservation Society, was formally adopted.

May 14, 1951, saw the Talyllyn Railway start running services using volunteer labour. More than two decades after the Southwold revival, it was the beginning of the British operational heritage railway sector.

Two years later, the hit Ealing comedy The Titfield Thunderbolt, which was inspired by the exploits of the Talyllyn Railway Society, told the story of villagers trying to stop their local branch line

from being closed, and brought the basic concept of volunteer-led railway revival into the public consciousness big time. On July 23, 1955, the Festiniog Railway, a one-time Stephens line reborn under the guidance of the late Alan Pegler, ran its first public preservation era train: the aim now was not to carry slate from the quarries at Blaenau Ffestiniog, as was the case when Stephens oversaw the line, but to satisfy a new public demand to see and ride behind, amid glorious Snowdonian scenery, what had become the transport of yesteryear.

STEPHENS: A FATHER OF PRESERVATION?

Three events in 1960 resulted in giant leaps for the still embryonic railway preservation movement. Monday, June 20, 1960 saw the Middleton Railway, a private freight-only concern to the south of Leeds that had operated continuously since 1758, became the first standard as opposed to narrow gauge line to be taken over and operated by unpaid volunteers, with students from Leeds University under the guidance of their lecturer the late Dr Fred Youell running trains as part of their University Rag Week charity events. Their very unorthodox passenger services comprised a diesel locomotive hauling redundant Swansea & Mumbles Railway double-deck tramcar No. 2… strong echoes of secondhand stock on a Stephens railway here?

Indeed, the original aim of the Middleton Railway Preservation Society was to find a home for their growing collection of redundant street trams, as opposed to running regular train services.

Local locomotive builder Hunslet loaned and later sold the society 1932-built 0-6-0DM No. 1697, named *John Alcock*, the first purpose-built diesel to work for a main line railway company, the LMS, which had ended up as the firm's works shunter. While the predominant image of the railway preservation movement is likely to be steam, 60 years on, many are surprised that the first standard gauge train of the heritage movement was hauled by a 'despised' diesel.

On August 7 that year, the Bluebell Railway ran the first train on the first section of the British Railways national network to be taken over and revived by volunteers.

Its first locomotive A1X 'Terrier' 0-6-0T No. 55 *Stepney*, had been bought second-hand from BR and was historically appropriate for a LBSCR.

The Bluebell laid down a blueprint for rail revival, but not necessarily one for plain sailing: indeed it was to be another eight years before the next former BR line to be reopened as a heritage line, the Keighley & Worth Valley Railway, would run its public trains.

However, opening at a time when BR was in the throes of implementing its

1955 Modernisation Plan to replace all steam locomotives with diesel and electric traction, it was able to save several classic locomotives that would otherwise have been lost forever. Furthermore, not all of the Bluebell Railway's locomotives were 'relevant' to the south of England; the first-ever appeal for funds to purchase a standard gauge locomotive for preservation was for the purchase of GWR 'Dukedog' 4-4-0 No. 9017, a veteran of the Cambrian lines in Wales. It came to the Bluebell in 1961 because at the time that line was the only place where it could run, and it has been there ever since.

Indeed, the modernisation of the national network provided the driving force behind the operational heritage railway movement, as the public realised that their long-beloved steam locomotives would soon disappear forever, making their last journeys to the scrapyard.

Not only are heritage lines run under the 1896 Light Railways Act, as were Stephens' lines, with – rare exemptions apart – a maximum speed limit of 25mph, but also, just like the colonel's railways, they rely on second-hand locomotives and carriages.

While many revival groups have the cherished goal of recreating their chosen line exactly as it was in the age of steam, with the 'correct' locomotives and rolling stock, compromises have necessarily had to be made. So many of our heritage lines ran their initial public trains with, say, an industrial tank engine hauling 'modern' BR Mk2. coaching stock. Historically incorrect by many a mile, but there again, so Stephens-esque!

The operational railway preservation movement might also be viewed as building light railways 'in reverse'. A closed branch line or other small piece of the national network is taken over, and then reorganised and worked under the provisions of the 1896 act, in some cases ending up running on an isolated section of track 'from nowhere to nowhere' (with the connections either side having been lifted) with the sole purpose, not of providing regular A to B public transport, but of showcasing saved steam locomotives and giving an eager general public the chance to ride behind them again.

The third major event of 1960 occurred on August 27, when the Lincolnshire Coast Light Railway ran its first public services. This 2ft gauge line was built by enthusiasts based in the east of the country who had been volunteering in the Talyllyn and Festiniogy revivals but found regular travelling to Wales in the west a burden, deciding to set up a line on their doorstep instead. In true Stephens style, they used second-hand stock which had its origins in the trench railways of the First World War, and afterwards used on the 23 miles of the Nocton Estates Railway, which transported potatoes, sugar beet and fertiliser across the

Taking the colonel's use of second-hand locomotives and carriages one stage further in the modern age is the Nene Valley Railway at Peterborogh, unique among Britain's major heritage lines in that it can accommodate stock from the wider Berne continental loading gauge. As such, it has used stock from Denmark, Sweden, France and Poland. Pictured is 1944-built Swedish B 4-6-0 No. 101 stored at Wansford on static display. ROBIN JONES

Lincolnshire Fens until road transport made it redundant.

What was the first railway to be built anywhere in the world by enthusiasts on a green field site – as opposed to reviving an existing line – linked the Humberston Fitties holiday camp near Cleethorpes to a point where local buses turned around. From the start, it provided 'real' public services as opposed to 'enthusiast' or heritage trains, and in 1964, 60,000 passengers were carried. The colonel might have been well pleased not only with such figures, but also the fact that the line had been built very much 'on the cheap'.

Roll on six decades of expansion, and today's heritage railway sector has long since earned a significant place in the nation's tourist economy.

The UK and Ireland have around 130 heritage railways with 450 stations over 550 miles – a sufficient total length to match the distance from London to Inverness. Around 10 million passengers travel on them each year, producing around £250 million to the leisure economy.

Each of them has, by their essential nature, so much on common with Stephens' light railways (and indeed, as we have seen, several of them are now heritage lines), that the colonel has been dubbed the 'father of preservation'. North Yorkshire Moors, Severn Valley, South Devon, North Norfolk, Great Central… today's fabulous heritage lines all have Stephens DNA lurking in there somewhere. In that respect, he may now be viewed with hindsight as having been ahead of his time, rather than running behind it, at the time when motor transport was slowly but surely making his rural railways irrelevant.

But… wouldn't the Weston, Clevedon & Portishead Light Railway have made a tremendous heritage line today had it survived, not to mention several of the colonel's other undertakings that have been similarly lost?

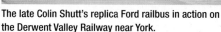
The late Colin Shutt's replica Ford railbus in action on the Derwent Valley Railway near York.

The East Wressle & Brind Railway's station with its sole motive power present.

THE EAST WRESSLE & BRIND RAILWAY

Where in the UK can you find a standard gauge railway wholly inspired by the light railways of Colonel Stephens, but one which he did not build? Stuart Chapman visits a private standard gauge railway in Yorkshire's East Riding and reports in words and pictures.

It is not the Kent & East Sussex Railway nor even the East Kent Railway, but there is a short standard gauge railway tucked away in the quiet countryside of the East Riding of Yorkshire not far from the small historic market town of Howden.

Wressle is a village on the eastern bank of the River Derwent and its parish includes the hamlets of Brind, Newsholme and Loftshome. In this remote and tranquil location you'll find an attractive little station, locomotive and stock, a short running line, where a small but dedicated group of friends meet most weeks to work on the railway.

The East Wressle & Brind Railway was the dream of the late Colin Shutt who sadly passed away in 2016. It all started back in 2004 when Colin decided to build a replica Ford railbus to enter into a competition. As we have seen, Colonel Stephens introduced two Ford railbuses

So Colonel Stephens in style – a gated crossing on the East Wressle & Brind Railway.

The interior of the station waiting room.

A 'freight' working using the line's only van.

The main running line consists of about 300ft of track running from the station alongside a field to a small wooded area. A single point just beyond the station leads back to the locomotive shed.

Modelled very much on a light railway and set among open farmland, the station is a beautiful wayside halt with a short platform and a single building consisting of a waiting room and ticket office.

Inside there is a wealth of Colonel Stephens related memorabilia on display including tickets, timetables, news articles and pictures. On a hook on one wall hangs the station master's cap while on another a clock keeps time.

A single semaphore signal stands at the end of the platform guarding a level crossing. The whole area is decorated with flowers in pots and hanging baskets reminiscent of a time when staff took such pride in their stations.

Motive power is provided by Ruston & Hornsby 48DS 0-4-0DM No. 371971. These locomotives were introduced in 1941 to replace steam in small locations and were easily operated by one man, making it ideal for the East Wressle & Brind Railway. A total of 204 were built up until 1967 and they were exported all over the world.

The railway's example was delivered new to Frederick Parker Ltd in Leicester in 1954 and worked for 15 years hauling aggregates before being withdrawn. In 1972 it was purchased by the Quorn & Woodhouse Action Group and was one of the first locomotives to work on the embryonic heritage era Great Central Railway.

The locomotive then moved to the Great Central Railway (Nottingham) at Ruddington before coming to the East Wressle & Brind Railway four years ago. The locomotive sees regular use either moving stock around or giving visitors rides in the cab. The only other item of operational rolling stock currently is a mess van converted from a Great Central Railway non-vent van built at Dukinfield.

Work on the infrastructure is now largely complete and the railway is unlikely to extend beyond its current limit. Work has been undertaken on the restoration of a plank waggon which when finished will display a 'Wressle Brickyard' logo.

Also stored in one of the workshops around the back is Wickham trolley No. 7516 which is in the collection of the Rail Trolley Trust and awaits long-term restoration.

The East Wressle & Brind Railway is all so idyllic, a real hidden gem, where out of the limelight a small group of friends just enjoy working together and keeping the legacy of light railways alive in this little corner of Yorkshire. The colonel would surely have approved.

into service on the Kent & East Sussex Railway in 1923.

The vehicle interiors were very much the same as a standard rural bus and could carry around 20 seated passengers. After a few minor teething problems they proved relatively successful and were introduced to other lines, including one to the nearby Derwent Valley Light Railway near York.

With the help and support of the Colonel Stephens Society, Colin built his replica railbus using some original components at his Yorkshire home, winning a commendation for his work.

The railbus obviously needed somewhere to run and that was the start of the East Wressle & Brind Railway. Having gone to great lengths to build the railbus, the attention paid to the railway was no less detailed with a beautiful small station and supporting infrastructure.

In July 2013, the Derwent Valley Railway, near York, celebrated its 100th anniversary with a special gala event and the replica railbus was one of the star attractions giving rides to the many member of the public who attended the event.

Just before he died Colin gifted the Ford railbus to the Colonel Stephens Society, and it was moved to the Colonel Stephens Railway Museum at Tenterden on June 5, 2017, for display, as we have seen, in a specially-built shelter alongside the museum.

However, this was far from the end of East Wressle & Brind Railway and with support of Elizabeth, Colin's widow, and the small group of volunteers, the line continues to flourish.